PETERBOROUGH FOLK

Peterborough Folklore

Francis Young

Lasse Press

First published 2017
by the Lasse Press
2 St Giles Terrace, Norwich NR2 1NS, UK
www.lassepress.com
lassepress@gmail.com

ISBN-13: 978-0-9933069-7-6

Typeset in Garamond by
Curran Publishing Services Ltd, Norwich, UK

Manufactured in the UK by Imprint Digital, Exeter.

Contents

Illustrations

Preface

Peterborough today is a large and expanding modern city that might at first glance seem an unpromising source of traditional lore and legends. Quite the opposite is true; located at the edge of the Fens and on the boundary between the ancient kingdoms of East Anglia and Mercia, Peterborough and its surrounding region (the Soke of Peterborough and the northern fringe of Huntingdonshire) is rich in folklore. Not truly part of Northamptonshire, Huntingdonshire or Cambridgeshire, Peterborough has its own distinctive stories to tell and its own individual customs and lore. It is my hope that, in addition to being of interest to local people, this book will be of wider interest to folklorists as a case study of English regional folklore.

Folklore captivated me from an early age, and as a child I collected a large number of books of fairy and folk tales from different European countries. My doctoral research in history drew me into the tangled relationship between official religion and supernatural beliefs in early modern England (c. 1500–1800) and thereby back into folklore. The stimulus for me to embark on this book was my discovery of the manuscript collections of the Victorian Peterborough folklorist Charles Dack in Cambridge University Library. Encountering a volume of Dack's unpublished manuscript notes and newspaper cuttings convinced me that a dedicated study of the region was amply justified, and examination of the secondary literature made it clear that the Peterborough region was neglected or glossed over in systematic surveys of regional folklore.

I am very grateful to Susan Curran for her support for this project and for bringing it to publication with Lasse Press. The staff of the Rare Books Room of Cambridge University Library, Peterborough Museum and Peterborough Archives and Local Studies Centre, especially Hannah Saunders, have been unfailingly helpful. I thank Virginie Ganivet for her insights on mummers' plays, Dr David Hall for permission to reproduce his image of St Vincent's Cross in its original position (Figure 18), and Chris Porsz for permission to reproduce his photograph of the dancers of Pig Dyke Molly (Figure 44). Lastly, I owe a huge debt of gratitude to my wife Rachel for her patience with research, insights on history and folklore, and willingness to walk or drive with me anywhere to examine and photograph local sites.

In quotations from John Clare's writings I follow the transcriptions adopted by his editors, except that I add punctuation in square brackets thus [.] where I feel it is necessary to aid the reader's understanding. Clare frequently omitted punctuation, and my insertion of it represents my interpretation and should not be taken as a definitive reflection of Clare's meaning.

The section of Chapter 2 on the Peterborough Lapidary is largely reproduced from the Introduction to my translation of that manuscript, *A Medieval Book of Magical Stones: The Peterborough Lapidary* (2016).

Throughout the book I refer to Peterborough Minster when the church building is meant, as this term was used by the people of Peterborough both before and after the Reformation, until very recently. The term 'minster' has the advantage that it can mean a monastic church, a cathedral or a large church of any kind; use of this term also avoids the anachronism of referring to 'Peterborough Cathedral' before 1541. I refer to the pre-Reformation institution led by the Abbot as 'Peterborough Abbey' and to the post-Reformation institution led by the Dean and Chapter as 'Peterborough Cathedral'.

All translations from Latin, Old English and Middle English are my own unless otherwise stated.

Francis Young
Serpentine Green, Peterborough
January 2017

Abbreviation

In the notes, CUL = Cambridge University Library.

For Helen

Introduction

> Superstition lives longer than books; it is engrafted on the human mind till it becomes part of its existence; and is carried from generation to generation on the streams of eternity, with the proudest of fames, untroubled with the insect encroachments of oblivion which books are infested with.
>
> John Clare[1]

The Soke of Peterborough,[2] a boat-shaped tract of land between the River Nene to the south and the River Welland to the north, has a special place in the history of English folklore. It was here that the great rural poet John Clare (1793–1864) was the first person in England to systematically record the customs, beliefs and traditions of his home village in the early nineteenth century. It would take many years for others to follow Clare's lead, and consequently his record of the folklore of the Soke of Peterborough is one of the earliest we have of any English region. However, in spite of its importance to the history of folklore, Peterborough and its environs have been somewhat neglected by folklorists, largely on account of boundary changes in the nineteenth and twentieth centuries. Northamptonshire folklorists have largely ignored the area as not really part of Northamptonshire, while Cambridgeshire folklorists have tended to overlook it as not really part of Cambridgeshire. This book aims to provide the first dedicated survey of the folklore of the area currently contained within the boundaries of Peterborough Unitary Authority, which includes the old Soke of Peterborough as well as parts of the ancient shires of Huntingdonshire and Cambridgeshire.

Charles Dack, the Victorian curator of Peterborough Museum who made a valuable record of the folklore of the city and its environs, observed in 1899 that 'Peterborough, the City of the Fens, has, I think, more curious customs surviving than any other city in England,'[3] while John Clare declared that 'it was impossible to go half a mile any w[h]ere about the Lordship were there had nothing been said to be seen by … old women or someone else in their younger days'.[4] The Peterborough region is dense with half-forgotten holy wells, supernatural apparitions, ancient fairs, macabre

---

1 Peterborough MS A34, p. 9, quoted on pp. 44–5 in George Deacon (1983) *John Clare and the Folk Tradition*, London: Sinclair Browne.

2 In historical sources the Soke of Peterborough is sometimes also called the Hundred (or Double Hundred) of Nassaburgh, the Hundred of Upton, or simply 'the Lordship', a reference to the authority of the Marquesses of Exeter as Lords Paramount of Peterborough. The city of Peterborough too has changed its name several times in its history, having previously been Medeshamstede, Burgh and Gildenburgh.

3 Charles Dack (1899) 'Old Peterborough customs and their survival', *Journal of the British Archaeological Association*, New Series 5, pp. 323–42, at p. 323.

4 John Clare (2002) *John Clare by Himself*, ed. E. Robinson and D. Powell, 2nd edn, New York: Routledge, p. 9.

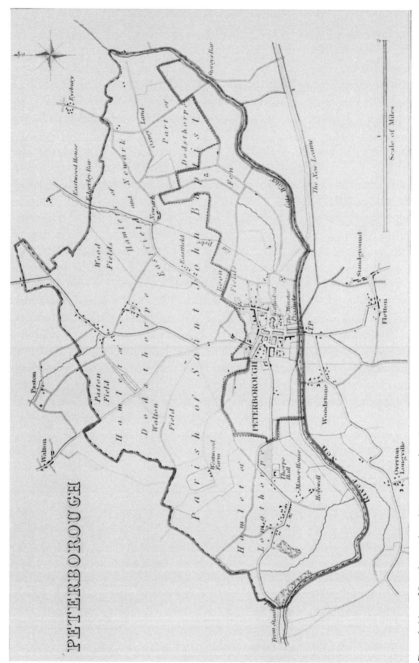

Figure 1 Map of Peterborough and its environs, from Samuel Lewis, *A Topographical Dictionary of England* (1835)

divination customs and tales of obscure saints unique to the region, such as St Pega of Peakirk, St Kyneburgha, St Kyneswitha and St Tibba of Castor, and the hermit saints St Tancred, St Torthred and St Tova of Thorney.

Before the arrival of the Great Eastern Railway in 1850 Peterborough seems to have been little more than an overgrown village clustered round a cathedral. Dack remarked that 'Peterborough, within the memory of many residents, possessed only about six thousand inhabitants',[5] and this may be no exaggeration of the city's size in the first half of the nineteenth century. Peterborough has changed even more dramatically in the intervening century or more since Dack wrote; the city's population in 2011 was nearly six times what it was in 1901. Yet already, in Dack's time, the city was changing; the brickworks had arrived and Peterborough was an important railway junction for the east of England.

Peterborough was for a long time the smallest cathedral city in England (a distinction now claimed by Wells). In 1652 Peter Heylyn described the city as 'a Town, unless for the Church, (that is, the Cathedral) of no great Esteem, as standing out of the way for Trade, and in no plausible Place for Health or Pleasure; yet shewing two handsome Streets, a large Market-place, and a fair Parish-Church'.[6] In the 1720s Daniel Defoe reported that of all cathedral cities, Peterborough was 'the least in England',[7] and the town had the name of a city only on account of the presence of the Cathedral. The entire city, together with numerous outlying hamlets, was a single parish until the mid-nineteenth century. The Great North Road bypassed the city, crossing the Nene at Wansford instead, and Peterborough's principal access to the rest of the world was by water at a time when the Nene was navigable to the North Sea. Until 1850 the Soke of Peterborough was a remote, obscure and very rural corner of England, cut off from Northamptonshire by the great Forest of Rockingham to the west and from East Anglia by the watery Fens to the east. It was a place where legends, superstitions and rural customs flourished.

City on the boundaries

Dack described Peterborough as 'the City of the Fens', but in another work he recognised that 'Being at a point where four counties are almost within a stone's throw, Peterborough possesses the traditions of the Counties of Huntingdon, Cambridge, and Lincoln, as well as Northampton.'[8] Peterborough has always, by virtue of its location on or close to so many boundaries, been a cultural melting-pot, and it is not possible to locate the city straightforwardly in any county. Since 1998 Peterborough City Council has had all the powers of a county council, but the area remains part of the 'ceremonial county' of Cambridgeshire (meaning that the Lord Lieutenant of Cambridgeshire welcomes the Sovereign to the city). However, Peterborough's associ-

---

5   Dack (1899), p. 323.
6   Peter Heylyn (1652) *Cosmographie* (London), p. 269.
7   Daniel Defoe (1748) *A Tour thro' the whole Island of Great Britain* (London), vol. 3, p. 29.
8   Charles Dack (1911) *Weather and Folk Lore of Peterborough and District,* Peterborough: Peterborough Natural History, Scientific, and Archaeological Society, p. 5.

ation with Cambridgeshire is recent; until 1965, the Soke of Peterborough (effectively a county in its own right from 1889) was ceremonially and traditionally part of Northamptonshire (as it had been since Domesday Book). In that year the Soke of Peterborough was merged with the county of Huntingdonshire, but the county of Peterborough and Huntingdonshire lasted for less than ten years before Huntingdonshire itself was merged with Cambridgeshire under the Local Government Act of 1974, taking Peterborough with it.

The present territory of Peterborough Unitary Authority includes all of the parishes that were once part of the Soke of Peterborough (although a small part of the Soke's territory, Stamford south of the River Welland, was lost to Lincolnshire in 1889) as well as two parishes from the ancient county of Cambridgeshire and five from the ancient county of Huntingdonshire. The northern part of the Huntingdonshire parish of Yaxley has also been absorbed by the Unitary Authority, and is the site of the continuing southward development of Hampton, although the village of Yaxley itself remains in the Huntingdonshire district of Cambridgeshire. Since the Unitary Authority includes parts of the old parish of Yaxley it is included in this book.

Once ecclesiastical boundaries are taken into account the picture becomes even more complex. Until 1541 the whole area, north and south of the Nene, was part of the Diocese of Lincoln. The creation of the Diocese of Peterborough in that year transferred the Soke of Peterborough (along with Northamptonshire and Rutland) to the new diocese while leaving Huntingdonshire, south of the Nene, in Lincoln diocese until 1837 when the Archdeaconry of Huntingdon was joined to the Diocese of Ely. The Church of England therefore divides the modern city in two, with all parishes south of the Nene in the Diocese of Ely and all northern parishes in the Diocese of Peterborough. The Roman Catholic Church considers the entire Unitary Authority part of East Anglia, under the jurisdiction of a bishop in Norwich.

For the purposes of this book, 'Peterborough' is defined as those ancient parishes of Northamptonshire, Huntingdonshire and Cambridgeshire now within the boundaries of Peterborough Unitary Authority. While this may seem incongruous – the Unitary Authority is, after all, a recent and somewhat artificial creation – these boundaries are now accepted and understood by most people living in modern Peterborough and its environs, and those boundaries still preserve – to some extent – ancient entities such as the Soke of Peterborough[9] and the longstanding links between the city and the Huntingdonshire parishes south of the Nene. Other additions to the Unitary Authority, such as the Cambridgeshire parish of Thorney, seem rather more arbitrary, as does the exclusion of the parishes of Alwalton and Farcet, which are still in the Huntingdonshire district of Cambridgeshire despite being more or less suburbs of

9   The Soke has lost one parish, Stamford Baron, to Lincolnshire. The parish once included all of Stamford south of the River Welland (the parish of St Martin), but today only the parish of St Martin's Without (the part of the old parish outside the boundaries of the borough of Stamford) is part of Peterborough Unitary Authority.

Peterborough. Similarly, the Unitary Authority boundary runs close to but excludes the site of the French prisoner of war camp at Norman Cross.

However, shifting boundaries are not new to Peterborough's history and the area has been subjected to numerous boundary changes since the sixteenth century. It is often on unstable geographical and geopolitical boundaries that the richest folklore can be found, such as in the Welsh Marches and the Scottish borders, and this seems to be true of Peterborough as well. Many people unfamiliar with the area may assume that Peterborough Unitary Authority is exclusively urban. Several ancient parishes and hamlets have indeed been swallowed up by the city's urban sprawl, but large rural areas also remain, especially in the north of the region. Furthermore, a number of villages manage to retain their rural character in spite of surrounding urban development, such as Longthorpe and the southern parishes of Orton Longueville and Orton Waterville.

Folklore

'Folklore' is an elusive concept that, according to the Folklore Society (founded in 1878) includes 'ballads, folktales, fairy tales, myths, legends, traditional song and dance, folk plays, games, seasonal events, calendar customs, childlore and children's folklore, folk arts and crafts, popular belief, folk religion, material culture, vernacular language, sayings, proverbs and nursery rhymes, folk medicine, plantlore and weather lore'.[10] This book is not so comprehensive as to cover all of these aspects of Peterborough's culture; for reasons of space, traditional sayings, folk medicine, plant lore and weather lore do not feature here, although much material of this nature was recorded by Charles Dack in his published works.

The Folklore Society also describes folklore more broadly as 'vernacular culture' – in other words, popular culture that is neither learned nor elite, and is created by, for and in the language of ordinary people. However, the boundaries of folklore are not clear-cut, both because elite culture often fed into the folklore of ordinary people and because elite culture drew upon folklore. Elements of folklore can be found in the poetry of Shakespeare, Milton, Spenser and many other great English writers. John Clare himself represents the most complex manifestation of folklore of all, since he belonged to the vernacular culture that created and consumed folklore, and yet he also recorded it and drew upon it for poetry that has become part of the 'elite' canon of English literature.

The folklorist, unlike the historian, is interested in stories *as* stories, and in the process of storytelling and transmission. The historian, by contrast, is interested in whether stories are evidence for actual events – something that does not matter in the study of folklore, where the important thing is *that* the stories were told. However, many of the critical processes involved in studying folklore are similar to those used in history. In the second half of the nineteenth century, in particular, there was a tendency for authors to invent traditions. Such inventions cannot be disqualified as

---

10 See the website of the Folklore Society, folklore-society.com, accessed 11 December 2016.

folklore *if* they were adopted by the population at large and became part of 'vernacular culture' and oral tradition, but it is important to understand the origins of folklore derived from print literature and not to assume uncritically that it arose from pre-existing oral tradition.

Local examples of folklore derived from Victorian printed literature are the tales about Hereward the Wake (themselves loose adaptations from medieval sources) adopted into folklore from Charles Kingsley's novel *Hereward: The Last of the English* (1866). Few people are aware of the extent to which Kingsley (who grew up in Barnack) embellished the historical sources about Hereward, yet there is no evidence of a popular tradition of stories about Hereward before Kingsley popularised him.[11] The popular 'folkloric' perception of Hereward derives almost entirely from Kingsley's novel, but that does not invalidate it as folklore. The relationship between folklore and print literature is reversed in the case of E. G. Swain's thinly fictionalised *Stoneground Ghost Tales* (1912),[12] which seem to have drawn on genuine folklore of the village of Stanground in order to create fiction; yet separating folklore from fiction in Swain's stories is well-nigh impossible, since no one else made a record of Stanground's folklore.

Folklore is an organic creation of the people which is continuously evolving, and the collections of folklorists from John Clare in the 1820s to Enid Porter in the 1960s are no more than snapshots of an ongoing tradition. In spite of the perception that folklore is ancient and immemorial – and in one sense it is – it is also continuously changing. Old stories are constantly being forgotten and new folklore is still being made. The enduring popularity of stories of ghosts and hauntings[13] and the ever-fertile tradition of urban legends about 'secret tunnels' are evidence of this,[14] and in recent years the theatrical company Eastern Angles has created new local stories for its Peterborough-based productions.[15] Yaxley's May Day procession, revived in 2013, is already a local tradition. This book is not and cannot be a comprehensive survey of all Peterborough folklore, because folklore, by definition, is the stories and customs that belong to the people and are told and enacted by them.

John Clare was an extremely early pioneer of recording the folklore of his native Helpston and other villages in the north of the Soke in the early 1800s, and it is largely thanks to Clare that an interest in folklore became part of the English Romantic tradition. Clare's work is so early that it pre-dates the term 'Folk-Lore' itself, which was coined in 1846,[16] and it was not until the 1850s that many others became interested in local legends and superstitions. This was perhaps a consequence of the

---

11   As noted by Enid Porter (1961) 'Folk life and traditions of the Fens', *Folklore*, 72, pp. 584–98, at p. 590.
12   E. G. Swain (2009) *The Stoneground Ghost Tales*, Cambridge: Oleander Press (originally published 1912).
13   For examples of these see Stuart Orme (2012), *Haunted Peterborough*, Stroud: History Press.
14   'Medieval Peterborough tunnels simply local folklore', *Peterborough Telegraph*, online edition, 20 July 2012, peterboroughtoday.co.uk/news/medieval-peterborough-tunnels-simply-local-folklore-1-4081570, accessed 13 December 2016.
15   *Eastern Angles in Peterborough: 2008–2016 and beyond*, Peterborough, 2016.
16   Theresa Adams (2008) 'Representing rural leisure: John Clare and the politics of popular culture', *Studies in Romanticism*, 47, pp. 371–92, at p. 381.

unprecedented change brought to the landscape by the railways in the mid-nineteenth century. When Clare was growing up in Helpston, unless someone was wealthy enough to own a horse their experience of the world was confined to the distance they could walk from their home village in a day, and this accounts for the highly distinctive customs of individual villages before the age of steam. The railways allowed rapid travel and began to blur the country's regional distinctions. At the same time, intellectuals were becoming interested in local folklore, and the railways (ironically) enabled both amateur and professional folklorists to travel the length and breadth of the country trying to collect the endangered stories and customs of the common people.

Folklorists soon discovered that the collection of traditional lore poses particular challenges. John Clare described some of the problems when he set out to make a collection of local folk songs:

> [W]hen I had sought after them in places where I expected [to] find them viz the hay field & the shepherds hut on the pasture – I found that nearly all those old & beautiful reccolections had vanished as so many old fashions and those who knew fragments seemed ashamed to acknowledge it as old people who sing old songs only to be laughed at – & those who were proud of their knowledge in such things – knew nothing but … sensless balderdash.[17]

The first problem Clare faced was knowing where to look for traditional lore – and he had the distinct advantage of having grown up in Helpston and heard these songs sung as a boy; many of the later folklorists were the product of the urban middle class with no first-hand experience of folklore at all. Furthermore, Clare notes the reluctance of older people, the possessors of the tradition, to share their knowledge for fear of ridicule. Anthropologists are well aware of the difficulty of getting people to share their authentic culture with an outsider, especially one whom they perceive as better educated or more knowledgeable than they are. Clare faced this problem even as a cultural 'insider'; the older people thought they might be laughed at.

A second problem faced by Clare was how to distinguish between a genuine folk tradition and what he called 'sensless balderdash'. It is not clear exactly what Clare meant by this term, but since he claimed this 'balderdash' was sung at county fairs it may be a reference to common popular songs of the day that were not part of a distinctive regional tradition. Clare notes that people were proud to share these popular songs – perhaps because they perceived them as more socially prestigious – but embarrassed to share the genuine folk tradition. Clare knew the difference, because he had been brought up locally, but a folklorist visiting a community from the outside could easily be led astray.

The 'golden age' of folklore collection lasted between the establishment of the Folklore Society in 1878 and the outbreak of the First World War in 1914, when many rural communities were changed irrevocably. Many local festivities and customs

---

17 John Clare, Northampton MS 18, quoted in Deacon (1983), p. 43.

were discontinued during the austere war years and not revived afterwards, and the romantic nationalism that had buoyed up folklore collectors before the War was tarnished by the conflict. George Deacon argued that 'mass education, the spread of cheap newspapers, the mass migration to towns, the decline of paternalist and hierarchical structures and their replacement by authoritarian and class-based ones' all contributed to the decline of the folk tradition during the nineteenth century.[18]

However, it is important to note that folklorists from Clare onwards have been inclined to nostalgia and a tendency to exaggerate the decline of the traditions they were struggling to preserve. Clare was convinced that the enclosures of the 1820s were the death of folklore, when this was clearly not the case. As late as 1969, Enid Porter, the founder of the Cambridge Folk Museum, was able to produce a comprehensive survey of Cambridgeshire folklore, much of it still derived from local informants.[19] It is hard to ascribe to any one cause the decline of traditional folklore in Britain, but rumours of the death of folklore may be exaggerated. People living in the same area are now rarely sharers in a distinctively regional tradition of stories and customs, but from the 1960s onwards strenuous efforts were made to revive and reconstruct folk customs and traditions, such as the Plough Monday straw bears of Huntingdonshire and the Fens which are now seen in several towns in the week after Epiphany.

Other traditional festivities have survived as part of children's culture, relegated by the Victorians to schools and playgrounds, such as traditional May Day celebrations. Charles Dack noted with disappointment in 1911 that Peterborough's traditional Christmas waits had degenerated into groups of children going from house to house shouting 'Silent night' into people's letterboxes and demanding money,[20] while Punch and Judy shows for children retained traces of the mummers' plays of an earlier era. The intense urbanisation of Peterborough makes such revivals more challenging, but by no means impossible. The urge to celebrate the spirit of place and the need to tell stories and locate them in familiar settings is surely basic to human culture, and remains as strong today as it has ever been.

Medieval beliefs

In the Middle Ages the boundary between official Christian belief and unofficial 'popular religion' or folk belief was porous and shifting. Church officials made strenuous efforts to suppress unacceptable beliefs as 'superstition', such as pilgrimage to St Laurence's well and the cult of the unofficial folk saint Laurence of Oxford, both located in the precincts of Peterborough Minster. Ecclesiastical proceedings against such 'superstitions' have left a valuable record of their existence. However, the church also accommodated popular religion to a remarkable degree, permitting the existence of other holy wells such as St Leonard's Well and Holywell at Longthorpe and encouraging belief in miracles. Even the monks of Peterborough

18   Deacon (1983), p. 13.
19   Enid Porter (1969) *Cambridgeshire Customs and Folklore*, London: Routledge & Kegan Paul.
20   Dack (1911), p. 19.

entertained beliefs potentially at odds with orthodox Christianity; it is not easy to see how the 'Wild Hunt' described by the *Peterborough Chronicle* in 1127 sat alongside conventional Christian belief, and the monks' interest in magic is shown by the contents of books in the monastic library such as the fifteenth-century Peterborough Lapidary.

There are some indications that medieval beliefs and practices survived the Reformation, lingering on in half-remembered or debased forms. John Hales's recollection that women used to curtsey at the pulpit in Castor church in the 1830s,[21] for example, may have been a lingering survival of the Catholic practice of genuflecting to the altar. Likewise, Charles Dack noted that hot cross buns were preserved in the house throughout the year to guard against fire, a belief associated before the Reformation with the consecrated host (which, like the hot cross bun, was imprinted with a cross).

John Clare recognised that the practice of 'sugar cupping' at East Well in Helpston was a relic of Catholic rites,[22] while the natural historian John Morton simultaneously dismissed the 'holiness' of wells whilst continuing to advocate their health benefits, 'owing to a slight Tincture that they have of ... Minerals'.[23] Similarly, the Catholic past lingered on in continuing commemoration of saints in folklore and customs, such as the stories told in eighteenth-century Castor about 'Lady Conyburrow' or 'Lady Ketilborough' (St Kyneburgha), and Peterborough's annual procession in honour of St Catherine of Alexandria on 25 November. Peterborough even embraced the cult of the new 'saint' Edith Cavell, who was educated in Peterborough.[24]

Symon Gunton and early modern antiquaries

The Reformation eliminated a great deal of the 'popular religion' associated with Peterborough, taking away the pilgrimages and the relics of the Abbey. However, the Abbey's buildings escaped the dissolution unscathed, unlike many others, because Henry VIII chose to turn Peterborough Abbey into a cathedral. Unfortunately, the occupation of the monastic buildings by Oliver Cromwell's troops in 1643 led to their wholesale destruction and defacement by zealous Protestants obsessed with iconoclasm.[25] However, the seventeenth-century antiquary Symon Gunton (1609–76), whose father had been registrar of the Diocese of Peterborough and who was himself both vicar of St John's Church and a prebendary of Peterborough Cathedral, collected a great deal of information on the Minster before the Civil War. Gunton's book on Peterborough, *The History of the Church of Peterburgh*, was edited by Simon Patrick (1626–1707), dean of Peterborough 1679–89, and published in 1686.

21 CAMUS (2004) *Five Parishes, Their People and Places: A History of the Villages of Castor, Ailsworth, Marholm with Milton, Upton and Sutton,* Castor: CAMUS Project. p. 349.

22 Deacon (1983), p. 284.

23 John Morton (1712) *The Natural History of Northampton-shire; with some account of the antiquities,* London, p. 283.

24 See Shane M. Barney (2005) 'The mythic matters of Edith Cavell: propaganda, legend, myth and memory', *Historical Reflections,* 31 pp. 217–33.

25 See K. Friis-Jensen and J. M. W. Willoughby (eds) (2001) *Peterborough Abbey,* Corpus of British Medieval Library Catalogues 8, London: British Academy, pp. xxxviii–ix.

Gunton's book was one of the earliest and most extensive antiquarian studies of an English cathedral, and is especially valuable because it preserves a record of the Minster and its precincts before the Parliamentarian destruction. However, Gunton also lived at a time before the onset of Enlightenment antiquaries' contempt, especially in the eighteenth century, for information derived from popular report or ancient custom. Gunton refers to a number of old customs which were practised either in his own lifetime or within living memory of when he was writing, and makes several appeals to 'common tradition' within the book.[26] Stories such as Gunton's account of the 'paschal pickerel' in the Minster's lost stained glass and John Aubrey's report of a miraculous healing at the tomb of Katharine of Aragon give an intriguing glimpse of the cultural significance of the Minster to the city before the Civil War.

John Morton (1671–1726), the rector of Oxendon, Northamptonshire, produced a 'natural history' of Northamptonshire, including the Soke of Peterborough, in 1712. This was a complete landscape history of the area, and inevitably for such a detailed study, Morton was compelled to rely on popular report and the testimony of local people. Morton's *Natural History* is especially valuable as a source for folklore associated with natural features such as wells and springs. The early antiquaries' intense interest in local traditions meant that they were often prepared to listen to the stories of ordinary people, and as a consequence they were often the first to preserve snippets of folklore. These snippets are often especially valuable because they date from long before the self-conscious collection and preservation of folklore began.

John Clare the folklorist

As well as being one of the great English Romantic poets, John Clare was a collector of folklore and, in particular, folk songs (which were the inspiration for much of his poetry). Had he not found fame as a poet, Clare would no doubt be celebrated as one of the founders of English folklore studies. Clare's manuscripts, including his records of folk traditions and customs and transcriptions of songs, are now part of the collections of Peterborough Museum. George Deacon argued that the importance of Clare's folk collections lies in '[h]is intimacy with, and commitment to, the life of his village contemporaries .... Clare records without pretension or condescension the spirit of a tradition of mutual and self-entertainment.'[27] 'Popular antiquarians' who were interested in local lore existed in the eighteenth century, but Theresa Adams has made the case that Clare was the first person in England to be interested in the social context of customs, and the first to collect folklore through fieldwork.[28]

Clare's papers are extremely valuable not only for the records of lore and customs they contain, but also because they reveal something of the process by which he became

---

26   Gunton (1686), pp. 3, 56, 164, 335 ('common fame'), 337 ('common talk').
27   Deacon (1983), p. 11.
28   Adams (2008), pp. 381–2.

aware of and collected folklore. In the first instance, Clare gleaned his knowledge from his parents:

> [M]y mother knew not a single letter, & superstition went so far with her, that she believed the higher parts of learning was the blackest arts of witchcraft, & that no other means coud attain them; my father ... was very fond of the superst[it]ious tales that are hawked about a sheet for a penny, such as old Nixons Prophesies, Mother Bunches Fairey Tales, & Mother Shiptons Legacy.[29]

The reliance of Clare's semi-literate father on broadsides and chapbooks for entertainment is a reminder that folklore was never (at least after the Reformation) an exclusively oral tradition, and was continuously being refreshed by the printed word. However, because literacy remained limited to a few individuals in most rural communities until the advent of compulsory education, it was up to these people to disseminate the stories they read orally, and this process of oral transmission lent itself to elaboration, embellishment and ornamentation. The printed word was highly valued in Helpston, so much so that some people believed everything in print was true. Clare recorded that one local man, John Billings:

> has a cupboard full of penny books[;] the king & the cobbler[,] Seven Sleepers[,] a[c]counts of People being buried so many days & then dug up alive[,] Of bells in churches ringing in the middle of the night[,] Of spirits warning men when they was to dye &c[,] each of the relations attested by overseers churchwardens &c of the parish w[h]ere the strange relations happened[,] always a century back w[h]ere none lives to contradict it.[30]

It seems likely, based on Clare's description, that Billings was in possession of old pamphlets and broadsides describing strange and wonderful providences, a popular genre in the seventeenth century. Clare's story shows that these apparently ephemeral products of the printing press were in fact treasured for generations, and no doubt made their way into oral traditions of folklore. However, Clare also learned directly from the oral tradition of illiterate people, such as 'old Mary Bains the cow keeper famous for the memory of old customs'.[31]

Cheap print was not the only external influence that renewed and informed popular beliefs in Clare's Soke of Peterborough. Deacon argued that Clare was well aware of 'the migrant nature of the folk tradition',[32] which depended not only on wandering 'bookmen' (sellers of broadsides) but also on Romany gipsies who made a living by musical performance as well as telling fortunes and selling charms and love tokens. Clare often visited the gipsy camp at Langley Bush near Helpston and learned

---

29   John Clare, Northampton MS 14, quoted in Deacon (1983), p. 22.
30   John Clare, Peterborough MS A25, p. 30 quoted in Deacon (1983), p. 37.
31   John Clare, Peterborough MS A18, p. 269, quoted in Deacon (1983), p. 23.
32   Deacon (1983), p. 13.

folk songs from them.[33] Even in the pre-industrial, rural Soke of Peterborough ethnic diversity was present in the community and enriched its folklore.

Clare's collection of the folklore of his native Helpston ultimately gave him material for poetry that was intended not so much for his neighbours as for the Romantic literary salons of London. Folklore and folk customs featured prominently in poetic works such as 'The village minstrel' (1819–20) and 'The rivals' (1827), but there was a price to be paid for Clare's success as a poet. Sarah Houghton has argued that, by the very act of recording Helpston's folk customs and using them in his poetry, Clare was sacrificing his ability to be an unselfconscious participant in those customs and became alienated from them.[34] Whether or not this is true, Clare's evocation of lore and customs is invariably nostalgic, and he was convinced that enclosure had destroyed or was destroying them. In retrospect, Clare's assessment seems unnecessarily gloomy, since many of the customs described by Clare survived into the nineteenth and twentieth centuries. It is possible, therefore, that Clare's adoption of an attitude of nostalgia was a means of dealing with the fact that his status as a mainstream literary figure had removed him from his own folk tradition.

Furthermore, although Clare remained to some extent a participant in the folk tradition, by his adoption of value-laden vocabulary in describing that tradition he consciously stepped outside it. In common with most nineteenth-century collectors of folklore he used the words 'superstition' or 'superstitious' to describe beliefs considered quaint, ridiculous or superfluous. It is unsurprising that he did so; although Clare successfully instated rural tradition and customs at the heart of English Romantic literature, he was also the product of an education system still rooted in the eighteenth-century crusade against 'superstition' in all its forms. All nineteenth-century British folklorists had to contend with an inherent contradiction between their fascination with local customs and lore, and the contempt for superstition that underpinned not only their education but also their class status.

Most folklorists dealt with the problem by adopting an attitude of patronising curiosity towards the customs of the common people. A good example of this condemnatory approach to folklore can be found in the *Peterborough Advertiser*'s 1911 account of the practice of watching in the church porch on St Mark's Eve (24 April) in Clare's home village of Helpston:

The whole thing has a distinct smack of the witch-finding period in England's History which originated in the latter part of the Sixteenth Century and flourished vigorously in the Seventeenth and Eighteenth Centuries because, as the 'Comprehensive History of England' says, the common people could no longer believe in Saints and miracles, they took up these various superstitions. They were the days of the Ducking Stool for witches (*sic.*), provided in each village, and worse than that they were the days of many

33   Deacon (1983), pp. 27, 300–1.
34   Sarah Houghton (2006) 'The "community" of John Clare's Helpston', *Studies in English Literature, 1500–1900,* 46, pp. 781–802, at p. 796.

innocent women being put to death on charges of having bewitched something or somebody.[35]

There were no grounds whatsoever for the author of this piece to connect the practice of watching in the church porch to witchcraft, other than the fact that it was 'superstition' and belief in witchcraft was the 'superstition' par excellence that formal education especially ridiculed and targeted for eradication.

As the nineteenth century wore on, folklorists' fascination with local customs increased but the government's interest in universal education – which included the elimination of 'superstition' – also grew. Furthermore, governments became progressively more concerned about the unruly nature of many annual customs; 'misrule', the temporary overturning of the hierarchy of society and suspension of law and order, was a key feature of many festivals, from the aggressive 'plough witches' of Plough Monday to the rebellious schoolboys of St Andrew's Day. It is unclear whether rural festivities actually became more disorderly in the nineteenth century or whether the authorities simply became more sensitive to what they perceived as bad behaviour. It is certainly possible that an increase in population, combined with cheaper and more readily available means of transport, did indeed result in more disorder at events like fairs and public feasts. However, Victorian authorities were also intolerant of any behaviour that challenged the immutability of class, and misrule gradually became unacceptable and was suppressed wherever possible.

The Fairs Act of 1873 was a key milestone in this process, allowing government ministers to suppress any fair by executive authority without the involvement of the Privy Council. Most fairs had originally been authorised by royal charters, which had made it extremely difficult to discontinue them until the advent of the Fairs Act (only the Privy Council can repeal a royal charter). Fairs were cherished annual events all over the country that boosted local economies, but Victorian governments perceived them as opportunities for drunkenness, sexually promiscuous behaviour, and the suspension of normal licensing laws regarding the sale of alcohol. Peterborough's major fair, Bridge Fair, survived the Fairs Act but was not immune from change. In 1905 the Mayor and Corporation of the city voted to discontinue the formal proclamation of Bridge Fair because it had become an opportunity for locals to make fun of them in public, and traditional mockery of figures of authority was no longer acceptable to middle-class Edwardian social sensibilities. Victorians and Edwardians loved folklore and traditional customs, but very often preferred sanitised and contained versions of them.

Charles Dack and Victorian folklorists

The folklore of the Soke of Peterborough, as part of Northamptonshire, received some coverage in nineteenth-century studies of Northamptonshire folklore by Thomas

---

35   'A weird local custom!', *Peterborough Advertiser*, 17 May 1911, newspaper cutting in CUL, Lib.5.89.520–1, p. 265.

Sternberg, Alfred Story and Charles Wise.[36] However, the city also had its own folk-lorist, Charles Dack (b. 1847). Dack was, like Clare, a man of fairly humble origins and, to a large extent, an autodidact. He was born at Holt on the north Norfolk coast and came to Peterborough as an employee of the Great Eastern Railway Company, in whose employ he remained while becoming assistant secretary (and subsequently honorary curator) of Peterborough Museum from 1880. One of the newspaper cuttings preserved by Dack contains a biographical sketch of him by a local journalist written in 1911:

> Charles Dack is a Norfolk boy, born in the later Forties and educated at Lowestoft and Peterborough, coming here at 12 years of age (1861). He was the only one of the family, indeed his grandfather was an only son, his father was an only son, and Charles Dack was an only son (and remains a bachelor). In 1864 he entered the G. E. R. [Great Eastern Railway] Clerical Service under his step-father, Mr. Norton, stationmaster, and remained an official until a couple of years ago (December, 1908). He is a man of many parts, and there is little worth knowing he does not know. Very few are aware he was an organist at Rev. Alex. Murray's Chapel (now Mr. Butler's) in Westgate for many years until 1880. He was originally a pupil of John Speechley, the famous Cathedral organist and F. R. Barratt, and as a Secretary to the famous Cathedral Oratorios in later years he was excellent. There is the antiquary and collector in every fibre of him. He can't help it. And that is just where he has been such a splendid hon. Curator to Peterborough Museum. When ten years old he started stamp collecting, the first one he had being a Mulready Envelope; then a presentation from an aunt of an Old China mug inspired him with Ceramics; no better amateur authority to-day on Ceramics than Charles Dack; Old Glass is a speciality of his (witness the lovely case on loan in Peterborough Museum), whilst Tokens and Coins absorb his leisure moments to an inordinate degree. But local topography and prints have a great space in his heart and head, and he has given of his best to Peterborough Museum in industry and experiences. He has the pen of a ready writer in the Archaeological line.

The *Saturday Citizen* noted that Dack was most proud of having raised £2,500 for the restoration of the west front of Peterborough Cathedral, and that 'there are heaps of things with which he is or has been associated for the good of the City which need not be mentioned in this short review'. However, the newspaper observed that 'latterly [he] has affected a little of the recluse – does not entertain, and contents himself with his books and his dog'.[37] One of the things the journalist chose not to mention was Dack's interest in local folklore, which led him to write an article entitled 'Old Peterborough customs and their survival' for the British Archaeological Association

---

36   Thomas Sternberg (1851) *The Dialect and Folk-lore of Northamptonshire*, London: J. R. Smith; Alfred T. Story (1883) *Historical Legends of Northhamptonshire*, Northampton: John Taylor; Charles Wise (1905) *Northamptonshire Legends put into Rhyme*, Kettering. Story (1883), pp. 1–18 gives a fairly detailed account of the legends associated with the foundation of Peterborough Abbey.

37   'Telephone talks – or, local notabilities rung up', *Saturday Citizen*, 14 January 1911, newspaper cutting in CUL, Lib.5.89.520–1, p. 269.

in 1899 and a short pamphlet entitled *Weather and Folk Lore of Peterborough and District* in 1911.[38] In the intervening years Dack contributed numerous short articles on folklore to local newspapers.

A volume of Dack's personally annotated collection of his own pamphlets, bound together with cuttings from the *Peterborough Advertiser* and other newspapers to which he contributed, is now held in the Rare Books Room of Cambridge University Library under the classmark Lib.5.89.520–1. The volume was purchased by the University Library from the Cambridge bookseller Gustave David on 18 February 1921, and it may have been bought by the bookseller after Dack's death.[39] None of his papers found their way to Peterborough Museum.[40] Unlike Clare's writings, Dack's published works offer few clues as to the methods he adopted in collecting folklore, but the *Saturday Citizen*'s comment that Dack had 'the collector in every fibre of him' would seem to be borne out by his writings on folklore, in which Dack made little or no effort at interpretation (or even organisation) of the material. This is in some ways a strength of the collection, since Dack did not overtly impose his own interpretations. Dack essentially collected snippets of lore from local people, although how he did this we can only guess at. As a museum curator, it is likely that he gathered a great deal from people who came into the museum to show him curiosities or share stories.

It is noticeable that, apart from a few mentions of amulets against witchcraft, Dack stayed away from the darker side of folklore, avoiding any material on witchcraft and ghosts. Whether it was a conscious choice on his part to avoid what might be labelled 'superstition' or whether people chose not to share such lore with Dack it is impossible to say. However, since Dack was not a native of Peterborough and, as curator of the museum, occupied a position with official status he was always an outsider (certainly to a greater extent than John Clare). Furthermore, although Dack may not have realised the irony of this, as a railway employee he had been brought to Peterborough by the very forces of change that were undermining the local customs he strove so hard to record and preserve.

Snippets of folklore were a common feature of local newspapers in the late nineteenth and early twentieth centuries; people seem to have been fascinated by the extent to which their society had changed within one lifetime, and had a great desire to preserve local folklore. Dack collected cuttings about folklore from Peterborough's two main newspapers of the time, the *Peterborough Advertiser* and the *Saturday Citizen*, some of which were written by him or derived from information he provided. Others, however, were supplied by other anonymous Peterborough folklorists. The late Victorian interest in folklore spread to the countryside, too, and an elderly resident of Castor, John Hales, delivered a lecture on the folklore, customs and traditions of the

---

38   Dack delivered a lecture containing the substance of the 1911 booklet to the Royal Archaeological Society in London as early as 1905 ('Curious local customs: Mr. C. Dack's fascinating paper', 12 April 1905, newspaper cutting in CUL, Lib.5.89.520–1, p. 78).
39   I am grateful to Liam Sims of Cambridge University Library Rare Books Room for this information.
40   I am grateful to Melanie Sockett of Peterborough Museum for this information.

village in April 1883.[41] Similarly, an account of old Christmas traditions by Thomas Ratcliffe published in the *Peterborough Advertiser* in 1908 is included in an appendix to this volume, although Ratcliffe never makes clear whether these were specifically customs of the Peterborough area or just general reminiscences.

W. H. Bernard Saunders's *Legends and Traditions of Huntingdonshire* (1888) was a fairly comprehensive survey of the folklore of that county, and included snippets of lore from Huntingdonshire parishes that are now part of Peterborough, including Orton Longueville, Bottlebridge and Stanground. Saunders also included a number of stories about the French prisoner of war camp at Norman Cross. Saunders's book was published in Peterborough and he acknowledged Dack as a source,[42] but stopped short of including Peterborough itself. Had Dack ever published an extensive tome like Saunders's then the folklore of Peterborough might be a lot better known; as it was, he confined himself to the publication of small snippets of lore in local newspaper articles and small, obscure pamphlets. Peterborough had its Victorian folklorist, but Charles Dack seems to have lacked the influence, financial backing and perhaps the interest necessary to produce a significant publication on the subject.

Contemporary folklorists

The prominence of folklore in Clare's poetry has inevitably drawn Clare scholars into detailed examination of the folklore and customs of Helpston, none more so than George Deacon, whose *John Clare and the Folk Tradition* (1983) is a dedicated study of Clare as a folklorist. Although Deacon's primary focus was on Clare's collection of folk songs, he also addressed Clare's collection of other folk traditions and their influence on his poetry. However, the separation of the Soke of Peterborough from Northamptonshire in 1965 led folklorists of that county to treat Peterborough rather summarily, if at all. Daniel Codd classed the city as part of Cambridgeshire, so it was not included 'in any great depth' in his book on Northamptonshire,[43] although he did choose to include the story of Werbode, the legend of Wansford Bridge, and the tradition that Oliver Cromwell's head was buried at Northborough. Peter Hill, similarly, includes a few traditions from the Soke in his *Folklore of Northamptonshire* (2005), but the coverage is far from comprehensive.[44]

Maureen James includes some tales from the Soke of Peterborough in her *Cambridgeshire Folk Tales* (2014), since the scope of her study follows the modern boundaries of the county. She briefly mentions John Clare's encounter with a will o'the wisp,[45] Peterborough's Wild Hunt[46] and the story behind Wyldbore's Day,[47] and

41   CAMUS (2004), pp. 348–50.
42   W. H. Bernard Saunders (1888) *Legends and Traditions of Huntingdonshire*, Peterborough: George Caster, p. xiv.
43   Daniel Codd (2009) *Mysterious Northamptonshire*, Derby: Breedon, p. 9.
44   Peter Hill (2005) *Folklore of Northamptonshire*, Stroud: History Press.
45   Maureen James (2014) *Cambridgeshire Folk Tales*, Stroud: History Press, pp. 62–3.
46   James (2014), p. 65.
47   James (2014), p. 45.

includes several stories concerning the Napoleonic prisoner of war camp at Norman Cross[48] as well as the story of the siege of Woodcroft Castle.[49] Jennifer Westwood and Jacqueline Simpson, in their important survey of regional folklore *The Lore of the Land* (2005), lump the Soke of Peterborough together with Huntingdonshire, following the rather controversial claim of Simon Jenkins that 'to most local people, Huntingdonshire and Peterborough still form a natural entity'.[50] Nevertheless, Westwood and Simpson include detailed accounts of the standing stones 'Robin Hood and Little John' at Castor, the ghost of Barnack rectory, the story of St Kyneburgha, the siege of Woodcroft Castle, the disembowelled knight of Orton Longueville, Peterborough's Wild Hunt, and, of course, the legend of Wansford Bridge.

Brian Jones's *Peterborough Book of Days* (2014), a miscellany of Peterborough history organised under each day of the year, also mentions a few local traditions,[51] while Stuart Orme's *Haunted Peterborough* (2012) gives a very thorough account of one particular aspect of Peterborough's folklore, its ghosts and hauntings. Most of the stories collected by Orme are anecdotes dating from the 1980s, 1990s and 2000s but some are older, culled from local newspapers, such as the Mayor's Walk poltergeist (1892), Woodston's 'woman in black' (reported in 1908), the ghost of Garton End (reported in 1926), and a haunted cottage at Upton (reported in 1920). While ghost stories arising from popular reports are undoubtedly folklore, not all manage to become folk tradition and survive beyond one generation – although, as Orme shows, local people still remembered and were interested in the Edwardian woman in black of Woodston as late as the 1970s.[52]

Structure of the book

Folklore rarely fits into neat categories and therefore it is always a challenge to organise the material for a study such as this. The first two chapters are thematic in nature, and address folklore that may preserve a memory of pagan beliefs and practices (Chapter 1) and stories of magic, miracles and witchcraft (Chapter 2). Chapter 3 then describes traditions specific to particular locations within the region, while Chapter 4 takes the form of a calendar of customs specific to certain days in the year. An appendix supplies the surviving primary source material on the mummers' plays once performed at Helpston, Yaxley, Milton and Peterborough, allowing readers to draw their own conclusions regarding the multitude of variations and differences in these folk plays as portrayed in the surviving evidence.

---

48   James (2014), pp. 122–30.
49   James (2014), pp. 181–2.
50   Jennifer Westwood and Jacqueline Simpson (2005) *The Lore of the Land: A Guide to England's Legends, from Spring-Heeled Jack to the Witches of Warboys*, London: Penguin, p. 357.
51   Brian Jones (2014) *The Peterborough Book of Days*, Stroud: History Press.
52   Orme (2012), p. 75.

Figure 2 A green man, traditionally interpreted as a pagan symbol,
from the porch of St John's church, Peterborough.
Photograph by the author.

Chapter 1

Paganism, Christianity and the legendary origins of Peterborough

The original establishment of Medeshamstede (Peterborough) Minster in 654–55 was, according to legend, accompanied by conflict between Christians and pagans even after construction of the monastery had begun. Paganism returned with a vengeance in the ninth century, when the original Abbey of Medeshamstede was burnt to the ground by the heathen Danes, not being re-founded as a place of Christian worship for a hundred years. Even after the definitive re-establishment of Christianity at the end of the tenth century, pagan traditions seem to have lingered in Peterborough, and the famous sighting of the Wild Hunt between Peterborough and Stamford in 1127 has been interpreted as evidence of the survival of folklore associated with the Anglo-Saxon pagan god Woden. As late as the thirteenth century the nave ceiling of the minster was adorned with a variety of pagan themes whose interpretation remains controversial, and it was necessary for the Bishop of Lincoln to suppress unauthorised well-worship with pagan origins in the Abbey precincts. For such a famous and ancient centre of Christianity, Peterborough has a surprising – if elusive – pagan past.

In the 'golden age' of British folklorists, before the First World War, there was often an uncritical assumption that the customs of ordinary people preserved pagan beliefs, because the conversion of England to Christianity had been only skin-deep in the Middle Ages and peasants remained essentially pagan. There is precious little (if any) evidence to support such a claim, but it remains the case that Christianity, in order to thrive in the pagan world of northern Europe, 'had to take on many of the trappings and some of the thoughts of the older cults'.[1] In other words, if we look for straightforward survivals of pagan worship into the Middle Ages we are likely to be disappointed, yet likely Christian *substitutions* for pagan beliefs and practices are common in the historical record. The material and spiritual needs of communities remained the same before and after conversion, meaning that the saints sometimes took on the roles of older gods. It is possible that Peterborough's saints – especially St Peter and St Oswald – sometimes played these substitute roles for earlier divinities. However, any discussion of paganism in England must always be tempered by the reflection that we know very few facts about Anglo-Saxon religion before Christianity, and identification of 'pagan' elements in later folklore is therefore always somewhat speculative.

---

1   Ronald Hutton (1991) *The Pagan Religions of the Ancient British Isles: Their Nature and Legacy,* Oxford: Blackwell, p. 184.

Figure 3 The foundation of Medeshamstede by King Peada and Abbot Seaxwulf, from a stained glass window in the south aisle of St John's church, Peterborough. Photograph by the author.

The coming of Christianity

Christianity formally arrived in Anglo-Saxon England in the year 597, when St Augustine landed at Ebbsfleet in Kent and converted the local king, Ethelbert. At this period the area where Peterborough now stands was a marshy zone between the East Angles to the east and south, the Angles of Lindsey (Lincolnshire) to the north and the Mercians to the west. The people who inhabited what later became known as the Soke of Peterborough were the Middle Angles, kinsfolk of the East Angles and the people of Lincolnshire and Northumbria.[2] South of the Nene lived the Gyrwe ('marsh dwellers'), 'all the South Angles who live in the great fen'.[3] The Angles originated in southern Denmark and Frisia, arriving in Britain towards the end of the fifth century and bringing with them their pagan beliefs. While the Angles of East Anglia, Lindsey and Northumbria were early adopters of the new Christian faith, the Middle Angles remained subject to their powerful western neighbour, Mercia, which was ruled from the late 620s onwards by England's last significant pagan king, Penda.

In 653 Penda made his son Peada king of the Middle Angles, since it was standard practice at the time to hand out sub-kingdoms to sons while the over-king was still living. Peada was converted to Christianity on a visit to Northumbria, where he married King Oswiu's daughter Ealhflæd. In 654 or 655 Peada founded a minster dedicated to St Peter as a centre of the Christian faith in his little sub-kingdom at a place called Medeshamstede. The Abbey of Medeshamstede was Mercia's first significant foundation, and the land on which the Abbey was built was given by a nobleman named Seaxwulf, who also became the community's first abbot and, later, Bishop of the Middle Angles.[4] Medeshamstede, later known as Burgh, would eventually become the city of Peterborough.

In November 655 Oswiu killed Penda at the Battle of the Winwæd, which meant Peada's promotion to king of Mercia. Peada himself died in 656, before the minster was complete, leaving both its completion and the governance of the kingdom to his brother Wulfhere (d. 675). The historical Wulfhere is remembered as a successful and powerful Christian king of Mercia, but a medieval monk of Peterborough, Walter of Whittlesey, presented Wulfhere in a rather different light. Walter compiled a history of Peterborough Abbey in around 1330,[5] and portrayed Wulfhere as an inconsistent promoter of Christianity, on account of the influence of his pagan steward Werbode. In Gunton's words, Wulfhere 'neglected his Vow, taking no care of Christian Religion;

2   'Middle Angles' in M. Lapidge, J. Blair, S. Keynes and D. Scragg (eds) (2000) *The Blackwell Encyclopedia of Anglo-Saxon England*, Oxford: Blackwell, p. 312.

3   Janet Fairweather (ed.) (2005) *Liber Eliensis: A History of the Isle of Ely from the Seventh Century to the Twelfth*, Woodbridge: Boydell, p. 4.

4   Sarah Foot (2006) *Monastic Life in Anglo-Saxon England, c. 600–900*, Cambridge: Cambridge University Press, p. 268.

5   On Walter of Whittlesey see Julian Luxford (2015) 'Intelligent by design: the manuscripts of Walter of Whittlesey, monk of Peterborough', *Electronic British Library Journal*, pp. 1–33, at pp. 2–9, bl.uk/eblj/2015 articles/article13.html, accessed 29 November 2016.

nor of erecting Temples, but committed many Impieties, so that the Chaos of Heathenism began to overspread all again'.[6]

The legend of Wulfade and Rufinus

According to one legend, Wulfhere's son Wulfade was hunting a hart one day, which sought refuge at the cell of St Chad, the apostle of Mercia. Chad saved the animal by hiding it with boughs and leaves, and when Wulfade came to find it Chad converted him to Christianity and baptised him. Wulfade then persuaded his brother Rufinus to become a Christian and Chad baptised him too. However, Werbode hated Wulfade and Rufinus because they had opposed his plan to marry their sister Werburgh, and betrayed them to their father. Wulfhere followed them to the place where they went to pray and killed them in an uncontrollable rage. Wulfhere and Werbode buried the bodies, but after the murder Werbode acted as though possessed by the devil, tearing the flesh from his arms with his teeth, until one day he was strangled by the devil in front of the king's house. This 'king's house' could have been any one of the royal palaces of Mercia, and Gunton seems to have been responsible for the claim that this happened at Peterborough, partly on the basis of local folklore concerning the well in the centre of the monastic cloister:

> In the Western Cloyster of the Church of Peterburgh (as shall hereafter be more largely related) was the story of this King Wolfere curiously painted in the Windows, and in the midst of the quadrangle of the whole Cloyster, commonly called The Laurel Yard, was there a Well, which common Tradition would have to be that wherein S. Chad concealed Prince Wulfades heart.[7]

The association between these legendary events and the cloister may have originated from the fact that a late medieval poem inscribed in couplets in the windows of the cloister told the story, here given in both the original Middle English and a modern English translation:[8]

---

6   Gunton (1686), p. 2.
7   Gunton (1686), p. 3.
8   Two transcriptions of the poem exist, one by William Dugdale from British Library MS Cotton A.V. in *Monasticon Anglicanum* (London, 1655), vol. 1, pp. 70–1 and the other in Gunton (1686), pp. 104–12. There are a number of differences between the two transcriptions (as well as minor differences of spelling); here I follow Dugdale's transcription but note any significant differences recorded by Gunton. Gunton, unlike Dugdale, specified which cloister windows contained each verse; however, given that Dugdale recorded slightly more verses than Gunton this may not be accurate. The transcriptions appear to be independent records by two different people made before the destruction of the cloister in 1643, although it is unclear whether the cloister windows survived the dissolution. See also Gordon Hall Gerould (1917) 'The Legend of St. Wulfhad and St. Ruffin at Stone Priory', *Proceedings of the Modern Language Association*, 32, pp. 323–37, at pp. 334–5.

Figure 4 Site of the Laurel Yard Well in the cloister of Peterborough Minster, traditionally where St Wulfade's heart was deposited by St Chad. Photograph by the author.

Historia de fundatione hujus coenobii, elegantissime in fenestris vitreatis, ex occidentali parte claustri ibidem depicta fuit, cum Anglicanis hisce carminibus argumentum ejusdem illustrantibus.

The history of the foundation of this monastery was depicted most elegantly in glass windows on the west side of the cloister of the same, with the argument of the same being illustrated with these English verses (lit. 'songs').

King Penda a Paynim as Writing seyth
Got these five children of Christen fayth.

King Penda, a pagan, as writings say,
Fathered these five Christian children.

Kyneburga and Keniswitha, as I reade,
Peada, Wlfer and Etheldred.[9]

Kyneburga and Kyneswitha, as I read,
Peada, Wulfhere and Ethelred.

The noble King Peada, by God's grace,
Was the first founder of this place.

The noble King Peada, by God's grace,
Was the first founder of this place.

By Queen Ermenild had King Wlfere
These twae sonnes that yee see here.

By Queen Ermenhilda King Wulfhere had
These two sons that you see here.

Wlfade went forth,[10] as he was wont
In the forest, the Hart to hunt.

Wulfade goes forth, as was his custom,
Into the forest the hart to hunt.

Fro all his men Wlfade is gon,
And suyeth, himselfe, the hart alone.

From all his men Wulfade is gone
And pursues the hart alone for himself.

The harte brought Wlfade to a well
That was beside St. Chad's cell.

The hart brought Wulfade to a well
That was beside St Chad's cell.

Wlfade asked of St. Chad
Where is the harte that me hath lad.

Wulfade asked St Chad
'Where is the hart that has led me?'

The Hart that hither thee hath brought
Is sent by Christ that thee hath bought.[11]

'The hart that has brought you hither
Is sent by Christ who bought you.'

Wlfade prayd Chad, that gostly Leach
The faith of Christ him for to teach.

Wulfade begged Chad, that spiritual doctor,
To teach him the faith of Christ.

St. Chad teacheth Wlfade the fayth
And words of baptisme over him he sayth.

St Chad teaches Wulfade the faith
And says words of baptism over him.

St. Chad devoutly to messe him dight
And hoseled[12] Wlfade Christ his knight.

St Chad devoutly celebrated mass for him
And gave communion to Christ's knight Wulfade.

---

9   This verse is missing from Gunton's transcription.
10   Gunton has 'rideth'.
11   This verse is missing from Dugdale's transcription.
12   Dugdale has 'shrived' (absolved of sin), but Gunton's 'hoseled' makes more sense here. Wulfade has just been baptised so requires no absolution.

Wlfade stayed with St. Chad that day	Wulfade stayed with St Chad that day
And bad him for his brother Rufine pray.[13]	And bade him pray for his brother Rufinus
Wlfade told his Brother Rufine,	Wulfade told his brother Rufinus
That he was christned by Chad's doctrine.	That he had been christened by Chad's teaching.
Rufine said to Wlfade againe	Rufinus said to Wulfade in return
Christned also would I bee fayne.	'I would also like to be christened'.
Wulfade Rufine to St. Chad brought,	Wulfade brought Rufinus to St Chad
And Chad with love of Christ him taught.[14]	And Chad taught him with love of Christ.
Rufine is christned of St. Chad, I wis,	Rufinus is christened by St Chad
And Wlfade, his brother, his fader[15] is.	And his brother Wulfade is his godfather.
Werbode Steward to King Wlfere	Werbode, steward to King Wulfhere
Told his sonnes both christned were.	Told [the king] that both his sons were christened.
To Chad's cell Wulfere gan go,	Wulfhere began to go towards Chad's cell,
And Werbode brought him hitherto.[16]	And Werbode brought him there.
Into the chappel entred the king,	The king entered into the chapel
And found his sonnes Christ worshipinge..	And found his sons worshipping Christ.
Wulfere, in woodnesse,[17] his sword out drew	Wulfhere drew his sword in a frenzy
And both his sonnes anon he slew.	And slew both of his sons immediately.
King Wlfere with Werbode tho	Then King Wulfhere, though with Werbode,
Buried in grave[18] his sonnes two.	Buried his two sons in a grave.
Werbode for vengance his owne flesh tare,	Werbode for vengeance tore his own flesh
The Divell him strangled, and to hell bare.	The devil strangled him and bore him to hell.
Wlfere for sorrow anon[19] was sick	Wulfhere was soon sick for sorrow;
In bed he lay a dead man like.	He lay in bed like a dead man.
Saint Ermenild, that blessed Queene,	St Ermenhilda that blessed queen

---

13   Gunton has 'Wulfade wished Seynt Chad that day / For his brother Rufine to pray'.

14   Gunton has 'Wulfade Rufine to Seynt Chad leedeth / And Chad with love of Faith him feedeth'.

15   Gunton has 'Godfather', but the meaning is the same.

16   Gunton has 'Toward the Chappel Wulfere gan goe / By guiding of Werbode Christys foe'.

17   The Middle English word used here, 'woodness', comes from Old English *wōdnesse* which is cognate with the name of the god Woden, and may originally have meant a frenzy or madness caused by the god. It seems unlikely that such a meaning could have survived into the late Middle Ages, however.

18   Gunton has 'burying gave'.

19   The word 'anon' is missing from Dugdale's transcription but the line scans better with it.

Councelled Wlfere to shrive him cleane.

Wlfere contrite shift[20] him to Chad,
As Ermenild his wife him councell'd had.

Chad bad Wlfere, for his sinne,
Abbies to found[21] his rewme within.

Wlfere in haste performed then
To build what Peada his brother began.[22]

The abbot Saxulfe, with his monkes there,
Did worship to king Wlfere.[23]

Wulfere indued, with great[24] devotion,
The abby of Burgh with great possession.

The third brother, king Etheldred,
Confirmed both his brothers deed.

Saxulfe, that here first Abbot was,
For ancoris at Thorney made a place.[25]

After came Danes and Burgh brent
And slew the monkes er they went.

Fourscore years and sixteene
Stood Brough destroyed by Danes teene.

Then Athelwold, the bishop of Wilton
Was mickle vext in contemplation.[26]

To build some cloister was his intent;
Yet where, or how, had no revilement.[27]

An angell appeared to him, by God's lore,
And bad him this place to restore.[28]

St. Athelwold to king Edgar went,

Counselled Wulfhere to make his confession.

Wulfhere, contrite, went to Chad
As Ermenhilda his wife had counselled him.

Chad told Wulfhere that for his sin
He should found abbeys within his realm.

Wulfhere then quickly accomplished
The building of what his brother Peada
     began.

The abbot Seaxwulf, with his monks there,
Did homage to King Wulfhere.

Wulfhere endowed, with great devotion,
The Abbey of Burgh with great possessions.

The third brother, Ethelred,
Confirmed both his brothers' deed.

Saxulf who was the first abbot here
Made a place for anchorites at Thorney.

Afterwards Danes came and burnt Burgh
And slew the monks as they went.

For ninety-six years
Burgh stood wrongfully destroyed by Danes.

Then Ethelwold, the bishop of Winchester
Was greatly vexed in contemplation.

To build some cloister was his intent;
Yet where or how had not been revealed.

An angel appeared to him, by God's word,
And told him to restore this place.

St Ethelwold went to King Edgar

---

20 Gunton has 'hyed'.
21 Gunton has 'build'.
22 This verse is missing from Gunton's transcription.
23 This verse is missing from Gunton's transcription.
24 Gunton has 'high'.
25 A reference to the ancient name of Thorney, Ancarig ('Isle of Anchorites'). An anchorite is a hermit, and the early monastery at Thorney was a collection of hermits' cells rather than a formal community.
26 Gunton has instead 'Seynt Athelwold was bidden by Gods lore / The Abbey of Brough again to restore'.
27 This verse is missing from Gunton's transcription.
28 This verse is missing from Gunton's transcription.

And prayed him to help his intent.	And asked him to help him in his intent.
Edgar bad Athelwold the work begin,	Edgar told Ethelwold to begin the work
And him to help he would not linne.	And that he would not fail to help him.
Thus Edgar and Athelwold restored this place,	Thus Edgar and Ethelwold restored this place,
God save it and, keepe it for his grace.	God save it, and keep it for his grace.

The prominent placement of this poem in the monastic cloister shows that by the late Middle Ages the local story of Wulfhere's change of heart had become part of the Abbey's foundation myth and a justification for the assignment of revenues and lands to the Abbey. The vernacular language of the poem and its placement in the cloister windows, at eye height, suggest that it was aimed at pilgrims rather than the monks themselves, and Dugdale's description of the poem's verses as *carmina* ('songs') even hints at the possibility that it was some sort of popular sung ballad (although the Latin word *carmen* could simply mean a poem). If the story of Wulfade and Rufinus has any foundation in historical truth at all, it is an indication that paganism did not die as easily among the Middle Angles of Peterborough as it had amongst their Anglian and Saxon neighbours. It is conceivable that the tale reflected a lingering memory of conflict between local Christians and pagans over the building of the minster.[29]

There is a curious coda to this story. The bodies of the martyrs Wulfade and Rufinus were supposedly buried at Stone in Staffordshire, but the Viking invasions of the ninth century destroyed records of miracles performed at the shrine. The procurator of the shrine set off for Rome in a bid to convince the Pope to include the two martyrs in the Roman martyrology (the church's official list of martyrs), and to aid his cause he took the head of Wulfade with him in the hope it would perform new miracles. The procurator proposed to the Pope that he be allowed to walk through fire with only Wulfade's head as protection, but the Pope refused, 'For the Sacred Canons did not appoint such trials by fire or water, nor decisions by single combat; but they were invented by superstitious men.' It is ironic that the procurator wanted to prove the sanctity of Wulfade, martyred by pagans, using the pagan method of trial by ordeal that survived in Anglo-Saxon England as part of the judicial system. However, Wulfade showed his displeasure with the procurator's presumption; the cleric left the head for one night in the church of St Laurence in 'Biterinum' (probably Bourges in France), and was unable to remove it in the morning. The head stayed in Bourges, and the procurator was forced to return to England without the relic.[30] The feast of Saints Wulfade and Rufinus is celebrated on 24 July.

---

29   There is archaeological evidence that at least one pagan practice – the burial of bodies accompanied by grave goods – survived at Peterborough after the coming of Christianity. An Anglo-Saxon glass bowl (now on display in the Cathedral Visitor Centre) was found in a re-used Roman stone coffin in the precincts of the monastery of Medeshamstede; see A. G. Vince (1990) *Saxon London: An Archaeological Investigation*, London: Seaby, p. 61.

30   J. B. Sollerio et al. (eds) (1727), *Acta Sanctorum Iulii*, vol. 5, Antwerp, p. 572.

Hereward and the white wolf

The Gesta Herewardi (*Deeds of Hereward*), a biography of the celebrated Anglo-Saxon warrior Hereward the Wake written by a scribe at the monastery of Ely some time between 1109 and 1131, tells how Hereward was tempted to sack Peterborough Abbey and burn the town. That very night Hereward receives a vision of an angry and splendidly dressed old man holding a key, who tells him to return the booty he and his men had taken from the church or die the next day. Hereward does so, but on leaving Peterborough Hereward and his men become lost in the dark Bruneswold.[31] However, a huge white dog (which turns out to be a wolf) and strange lights 'like those which are commonly called fairy lights' (*velut illae quae vulgus appellant candela nympharum*) appear on the soldiers' lances in the wood and guide them to the edge of Stamford (*ultra Stanford*), where the enchanted lights and the mysterious wolf disappear and Hereward and his men give thanks to God.[32]

The appearance of these obviously mythological elements in what is supposed to be a historical narrative of Hereward's life leads Joanna Huntington to observe that the story sits 'at the intersection of fiction and history', with elements redolent of romance.[33] Aleksander Pluskowski notes that 'this motif of a benevolent wolf has been associated with the local cult of St. Edmund, and perhaps earlier local emblematic uses of the wolf'.[34] The wolf was the sacred animal of the Norse god Odin – and, in all probability, of his English analogue Woden as well.[35] The cult of St Edmund, which was associated with wolves because the martyred king of East Anglia's head was found cradled in the paws of a wolf after his death in 869, was not especially local to Peterborough (it was focused on the abbey of Bury St Edmunds in faraway Suffolk).

However, as Rebecca Pinner has shown, the association of St Edmund with the wolf tapped into a much earlier stratum of East Anglian identification with the wolf as the totemic animal of the Wuffing dynasty (descended from Woden via Wuffa). Pinner also notes that St Edmund's wolf may have become an emblem of resistance to the Danes.[36] This may provide a better way of understanding the wolf in Hereward's story than any direct association with the cult of St Edmund; perhaps the wolf has become in this story a symbol of English resistance to the Normans. On the other hand, it is possible that the author of the *Gesta* simply chose a wolf as a suitable forest

---

31   The lost Forest of Bromswold, which gives its name to Leighton Bromswold in Huntingdon-shire and Newton Bromswold in Northamptonshire, once covered a vast area and stretched across Northamptonshire, Huntingdonshire and Cambridgeshire.

32   T. D. Hardy and C. T. Martin (eds) (1888) *Gesta Herwardi incliti exulis et militis,* in Geoffroy Gaimar, *Lestorie des Engles,* London: HMSO, vol. 1, p. 396.

33   Joanna Huntington (2013) '"The quality of his virtus proved him a perfect man": Hereward "the Wake" and the representation of lay masculinity', pp. 77–93 in P. H. Cullum and K. J. Lewis (eds), *Religious Men and Masculine Identity in the Middle Ages,* Woodbridge: Boydell Press, at p. 79.

34   Aleksander Pluskowski (2006) *Wolves and Wilderness in the Middle Ages,* Woodbridge: Boydell Press, p. 187.

35   A bearded figure often identified as Woden is depicted standing between two wolves on the cloisonné purse lid that is part of the Sutton Hoo treasure. For a discussion of the 'man between beasts' image see Rebecca Pinner (2015) *The Cult of St Edmund in Medieval East Anglia,* Woodbridge: Boydell & Brewer, pp. 222–4

36   See Pinner (2015), pp. 222–4.

Figure 5
Fighting warriors
of the Norman
Conquest era
on the font of
St Mary the
Virgin,
Wansford.
Photograph by
the author.

animal, but this does not explain why the wolf is set apart as unusual (and possibly supernatural) by its white colour. The *Gesta* do not explicitly identify the angry old man as the Abbey's patron St Peter (although this interpretation was later adopted), and Hereward's vision could be seen as an unwitting Christianisation of a dream-vision of the god Woden who subsequently sends his totemic animal, the wolf, to guide the English warriors to safety.[37]

---

37   The story of Hereward's escape from the Bruneswold was elaborated in Charles Kingsley's hugely popular fictionalisation of Hereward's story, *Hereward: The Last of the English* (Boston, Mass.: Ticknor & Fields, 1866), pp. 255–6.

The Wild Hunt

Perhaps the best known of all supernatural stories from Peterborough is the dramatic account given by the *Peterborough Chronicle* of the so-called 'Wild Hunt', which was seen around Peterborough in 1127. The Wild Hunt is a recurring theme of European folklore, as defined by Anne Rooney: 'The traditional Wild Hunt motif concerns a fiendish huntsman, sometimes with many followers and a pack of hellish hounds, who hunts the sinful, or damned souls, or unfortunate individuals who cross his path.'[38] In different parts of Europe, the hunter may be identified as Diana, Odin, Herodias or Satan, but in England the best-known leader of the Wild Hunt (in Windsor Great Park) is the horned Herne the Hunter, who earns a mention in Shakespeare's play *The Merry Wives of Windsor*. Nevertheless, the Peterborough account of the Wild Hunt is the earliest in England.

In the twelfth century Peterborough Abbey was renowned for its conservatism and insistence on adhering to Anglo-Saxon customs, long after the Norman Conquest of 1066. Hereward the Wake, the principal English rebel against Norman rule, had been knighted by the abbot of Peterborough (his uncle Brand), but the main way in which the monks defied the Normanisation of England was by insisting on writing in English rather than Latin or Norman French. This was at a time when the English language was being squeezed out of use by anyone other than the illiterate common people. Norman French was the language of the court and of knights, as well as the *lingua franca* of most monasteries (at a time when bishops and abbots were usually Norman aristocrats), while the Normans encouraged the exclusive use of Latin as a learned language, in contrast to the Anglo-Saxon tradition of writing in Old English. In spite of the fact that construction of a new Norman church began at Peterborough in 1118, the monks clung to the English language, and the *Peterborough Chronicle* (in which the Wild Hunt was recorded) was the only monastic chronicle still being written in English when it came to an end in 1154, nearly a century after the Conquest.

The events that led up to the sighting of the Wild Hunt in Peterborough were part of the ongoing struggle between the English monks and the Norman abbots who were imposed on them. One such abbot was Henry de Angeli who, in common with many Norman churchmen, was more interested in farming the revenues of the abbey than acting as a spiritual leader. The *Chronicle* was scathing of Henry, declaring that at the abbey 'he lived exactly as drones do in a hive – all that the bees drag toward them the drones devour and drag away'. However, Henry also brought supernatural evil with him, which began shortly after his arrival:

> Soon thereafter many men saw and heard many hunters hunting. The hunters were black and large and hideous and their hounds all black and broad-eyed and hideous, and they rode on black horses and on black bucks. This was seen in the park itself in the town of Burgh and in all the woods that stretched from the same town to Stamford, and the monks heard the horns blowing that they blew in the night. Trustworthy men, who

---

38   Anne Rooney (1993) *The Hunt in Middle English Literature*, Cambridge: D. S. Brewer, p. 34.

noticed them at night, said from the way it seemed to them that there were probably about twenty or thirty horn-blowers. This was seen and heard from the time he arrived there all spring up to Easter.[39]

The Wild Hunt in the *Peterborough Chronicle*, as well as being the earliest English record of the phenomenon, is also the only example in England where the Wild Hunt seems to be pursuing someone living rather than someone dead.[40] However, it is far from certain that the hunters are meant to be pursuing Abbot Henry (an interpretation derived from the function played by the hunters in other folktales). Nowhere does the chronicler suggest that Abbot Henry is the victim of the hunters; rather, it sounds more like Henry's evil has brought the demonic hunters with him, or else they are a monstrous omen of evil about the befall the monastery. Furthermore, there is no suggestion in the Peterborough account that the Wild Hunt is seen in the sky, nor is it associated with storms as in other legends.

For the folklorist Katharine Briggs, the *Peterborough Chronicle*'s account of the Wild Hunt set the pattern for later English folklore about the 'host of the dead'. Such stories usually involve someone coming across a band of riders that includes friends who have recently died. Briggs argued that the 'host of the dead' was essentially the same as the 'trooping fairies' also encountered in British and Irish folklore, since 'the distinction between the fairies and the dead is vague and shifting'.[41] Briggs detected three kinds of supernatural rides. First there is 'the true Host of the Dead ... following as a rule some god-like leader, who later becomes the Devil'; second, 'There are the euhemerized[42] gods, who are supposed to be wicked huntsmen, compelled to lead their hounds forever'; and third there is the 'Fairy Rade', usually found in Scotland and Ireland, which is a less sinister troop of beautiful fairies.[43]

However the Peterborough Wild Hunt does not fit neatly into Briggs's scheme, since the leader of the hunt is not identified and it is associated with a living rather than a dead man; nor is there any suggestion that the riders are the souls of the dead. A twelfth-century encounter described by Gerald of Wales may shed more light on

---

39   See C. Clark (ed.) (1958) *The Peterborough Chronicle, 1070–1154*, Oxford: Oxford University Press, p. 50: 'Þa son þæræfter þa sægon & herdon fela men feole huntes hunten. a huntes wæron swarte & micele & laðlice, & her hundes ealle swarte & bradegede & laðlice, & hi ridone on swarte hors & on swarte bucces. Þis wæs segon on þe selue derfald in þa tune on Burch & on ealle þa wudes da wæron fram þa selua tune to Stanforde; & þa muneces herdon ða horn blawen þet he blawen on nihtes. Soðfeste men heom kepten on nihtes; sæidon, þes þe heom þuhte, þet þær mihte wel ben abuton twenti oder þritti hornblaweres. Þis wæs sægon & herd fram þet he þider com eall þet lente[n]id onan to Eastren'. A translation of the passage can be found in H. A. Rositzke (ed. and trans.) (1951) *The Peterborough Chronicle*, New York: Columbia University Press, p. 154.

40   Rooney (1993), p. 35. For a discussion of the theme of the Wild Hunt in medieval English literature see pp. 34–9.

41   Katharine Briggs (2002) *The Fairies in Tradition and Literature,* London: Routledge (originally published 1967), p. 62.

42   Euhemerisation takes place when a story formerly featuring a god is retold so that the god becomes an ordinary man or woman.

43   Briggs (2002), pp. 64–5.

the Peterborough story than other Wild Hunt legends can. Gerald met a seer called Meilyr at Caerleon in South Wales who claimed to be able to see demons invisible to everyone else. Meilyr told Gerald that the demons were dressed as huntsmen, carrying horns, because they were hunting people's souls.[44] It seems highly likely that the monastic chronicler intends the huntsmen he describes to be interpreted as demons,[45] who are probably portrayed as huntsmen for exactly the same reason given by Meilyr.

It may also be significant that the location of the Wild Hunt specified in the *Peterborough Chronicle* – the woods between Peterborough and Stamford – is one and the same place as the 'Bruneswold' between Peterborough and Stamford where Hereward got lost with his men (according to the twelfth-century *Gesta Herewardi*) and was guided by a friendly wolf and fairy lights. Although wolves are not mentioned in the *Peterborough Chronicle*'s account of the Wild Hunt, the appearance of two folkloric motifs associated with Woden – the wolf and the Wild Hunt – in the same location in two separate texts seems more than a coincidence. Two local place names also recall the god – Woodston, just southwest of Peterborough on the opposite side of the Nene was *Wodestun*, 'Woden's town' in Domesday Book, and the probable meaning of Wansford is 'Woden's ford'.[46]

If indeed this is more than a coincidence, then the possibility arises that, in the twelfth century, the woods between Peterborough and Stamford remained associated (in however vague and half-remembered a fashion) with the pre-Christian English gods. An alternative (but not incompatible) interpretation is to see the strange riders of Peterborough's Wild Hunt as fairy or elf riders, an interpretation supported by Briggs's analysis of Wild Hunt folklore. Fairies are also alluded to in the Hereward story, where the word *nymphae* was the closest the scribe could come to rendering the English idea of elves or fairies.[47] Both stories would seem to imply that the woods between Peterborough and Stamford were believed to be a place of access to the fairy realm.[48]

However, it not certain that the Wild Hunt should be associated with Woden. In the 1960s the *Peterborough Chronicle*'s account was at the centre of a dispute between two folklorists, John Sprott Ryan and Audrey Meaney, over whether there really was

---

44   Gerald of Wales (1978) *The Journey through Wales and the Description of Wales,* trans. L. Thorpe, Harmondsworth: Penguin, pp. 116–20.

45   It was typical for Christian writers of the period to see all supernatural activity as the activity of demons.

46   Allan Bunch and Mary Liquorice (1990) *Parish Churches in and around Peterborough,* Cambridge: Cambridgeshire Books, p. 42.

47   On *nymphae* as a synonym for Old English *ælfenne* (female elves/fairies) see Alaric Hall (2007) 'Glosses, gaps and gender: the rise of female elves in Anglo-Saxon culture', pp. 139–70 in M. Risannen, M. Hintikka, L. Kahlas-Tarkka and R. McConchie (eds), *Change in Meaning and the Meaning of Change: Studies in Semantics and Grammar from Old to Present-day English,* Helsinki: Société Néophilologique, at pp. 146–7.

48   In contrast to many other English regions, allusions to the fairies in later Peterborough folklore are rare, although John Clare occasionally refers to them as 'doxeys' (see John Clare (1996–2003) *Poems of the Middle Period: 1822–1837,* ed. E. Robinson, D. Powell and P. M. S. Dawson, 5 vols, Oxford: Clarendon; vol. 5, p. 582n.). On one occasion he recorded that 'an old cow woman or herd woman' (presumably Mary Bains) once told him that sallow palms were called 'Cats & kittlings' because the fairies turned them into cats 'when they feasted in the pastures on summer nights' (Anne Barton (1999) 'Clare's animals: the wild and the tame', *Journal of the John Clare Society* ,18 pp. 5–22, at p. 7).

any evidence for Woden in Old English literature. Ryan thought that there was, and argued that the Old English 'Storm Riddle' was an allusion to the Wild Hunt:

It is the greatest of uproars, of noises over cities – dark creatures, hastening over men, sweat fire, and crashes move, dark with mighty din, above the multitudes; they march in battle, they pour dark pattering wet from their bosom, moisture from their wombs. The dread legion moves in battle. Terror arises.[49]

Ryan also saw an allusion to the Wild Hunt in an Old English charm 'against sudden stitch in the side' (the Old English charms are one of the few places where Woden is mentioned by name): 'Loud were they, lo, loud when they rode over the Hill. Resolute were they when they rode over the lands'.[50] However, Ryan regarded the Peterborough Wild Hunt as the 'version perhaps most close to what we imagine to be the nature of the Wild Hunt, as known in England – although we must allow for later influences'.[51]

Meaney rejected Ryan's approach, which interpreted the Peterborough Wild Hunt as analogous to Wild Hunts in Scandinavia and Germany led by Odin/Othin, pointing out that the Peterborough story was a post-Conquest one even if it happened to be written in Old English:

We have next to nothing to tell us if the idea of the Wild Hunt or of the Lost Souls was developed in England at all before the Norman Conquest, and if it did, what form it took – the *Old English Storm Riddle* is certainly atmospheric, but it is hardly clear, and need be no more than the product of poetic imagination. The description of the Wild Hunt in the *Peterborough Chronicle* is of no help at all in illuminating ideas current as much as five hundred years, and two foreign invasions, earlier. And if we cannot even be certain that the idea of the lost souls sweeping along in the storm, or of the Wild Hunt, was current in Anglo-Saxon England at all, how much less certain can we be that popular imagination made Woden its leader.[52]

Meaney was, of course, correct that the Peterborough account neither mentions a leader of the hunt nor identifies the riders as lost souls; and even if what the *Chronicle* describes is derived from other folklore of the Wild Hunt, this is evidence of Continental influence on English folklore. Henry de Angeli and his fellow Normans may have brought the Wild Hunt with them in more ways than one.

Kathleen Herbert put forward a more pragmatic explanation of the Peterborough Wild Hunt, suggesting that the huntsmen could have been 'a band of dissidents', following the example of Hereward the Wake and adopting 'blackened faces or masks'. She supports this theory by appealing to Tacitus's account of a Germanic tribe called

---

49   Quoted in J. S. Ryan (1963) 'Othin in England: Evidence from the poetry for a cult of Woden in Anglo-Saxon England', *Folklore*, 74, pp. 460–80, at p. 473.
50   Quoted in Ryan (1963), p. 473.
51   Ryan (1963), p. 473.
52   A. L. Meaney (1966) 'Woden in England: a reconsideration of the evidence', *Folklore*, 77, pp. 105–15, at p. 114.

the Harii, who would paint their shields and bodies black and attack in the middle of the night, giving them the appearance of 'an army of the dead', and suggests that the Harii could have been 'a cult association of warriors dedicated to Woden'.[53] These are intriguing speculations, but sadly unproveable.

Another approach might be to interpret the Wild Hunt as a dream experience. The chronicler notes that 'the monks heard the horns blowing that they blew in the night', even though the *Chronicle* apparently presents the Wild Hunt as something witnessed by waking people. Ronald Hutton has noted that in many parts of Europe, people believed they were snatched away in their sleep to be part of a 'nocturnal cavalcade' led by Herne, Herla, Diana or Herodias, and such beliefs were a matter of such concern to the church that a specific canon was drawn up in around 900 to condemn belief in nocturnal rides.[54] The Italian historian Carlo Ginzberg, in his book *The Night Battles* (1966), advanced an influential argument that belief in night rides led eventually to the idea of witches flying to the witches' Sabbath.[55] The Wild Hunt hovered at the borders between sleep and waking, between the worlds of the living and the dead, and at the boundary between pagan and Christian belief; in the Wild Hunt 'a transition from pagan beliefs to Christianity is hard to discern, if it exists indeed'.[56] The *Peterborough Chronicle*'s account of the Wild Hunt remains an intriguing but enigmatic glimpse into a world of twelfth-century supernatural beliefs about which we can do little more than speculate.

The arm of St Oswald

Ælfsige, Abbot of Peterborough 1006–42, acquired many relics for the monastery including the Abbey's most important relic up to the Reformation, the incorrupt arm of St Oswald. It was somewhat ironic that this relic became the main draw for pilgrims to Peterborough, given that King Oswald of Northumbria had been killed in 641 by Penda, the pagan father of King Peada of Mercia who founded Medeshamstede in the first place. St Oswald's incorrupt arm was originally given by King Oswy of Northumbria to the church of St Peter at Bamburgh in Yorkshire. At some point in the late tenth or early eleventh centuries the arm found its way to Peterborough – stolen, according to William of Malmesbury, by the Peterborough monks. The arm was certainly at Peterborough by 1060.[57] Such 'pious thefts' were not uncommon, and the acquisition gave Peterborough a relic to compete with the incorrupt bodies of St Etheldreda at Ely and St Edmund at Bury St Edmunds. Gunton, paraphrasing Bede, explained why Oswald's arm would never decay:

53   Kathleen Herbert (1994) *Looking for the Lost Gods of England,* Swaffham: Anglo-Saxon Books, pp. 38–9.
54   Hutton (1991), pp. 307–8; Ludo Milis (2012) 'The spooky heritage of ancient paganisms', pp. 1–18 in C. Steel, J. Marenbon and W. Verbeke (eds), *Paganism in the Middle Ages: Threat and Fascination,* Leuven, Netherlands: Leuven University Press, at pp. 5–7.
55   See Carlo Ginzberg (1983) *The Night Battles: Witchcraft and Agrarian Cults in the Sixteenth and Seventeenth Centuries,* London: Routledge & Kegan Paul.
56   Milis (2012), p. 7.
57   Jack Higham (1988) 'The Cult of St. Oswald at Peterborough', *Peterborough's Past*, 3, pp. 15–22, at p. 17.

Figure 6 The 'vice' and spyhole for the horuspex in St Oswald's chapel, Peterborough Minster. Photograph by the author.

Oswald King of Northumberland was very free and liberal in giving of alms to the poor; and one day whilst he sate at meat, one of his servants told him of a great number of poor people come to his gate for relief; whereupon King Oswald sent them meat from his own table, and there not being enough to serve them all, he caused one of his silver dishes to be cut in pieces, and to be distributed amongst the rest; which Aydanus a Bishop, (who came out of Scotland to convert, and instruct those Northern parts of England) beholding, took the King by the right hand, saying, *nunquam inveterascat haec manus*, let this hand never wax old, or be corrupted: which came to pass.[58]

However, in addition to being an important Christian relic, the legend surrounding St Oswald's arm had a distinctly pagan flavour as well. After killing Oswald, Penda had the king's head, hands and forearms hacked off and displayed on a pole. This can either be interpreted as a human sacrifice to Woden or as the creation of a 'pole of disgrace' to shame Oswald and replace the cross which Oswald had raised.[59] Subsequent legends told how St Oswald's right arm was picked up by a raven (the bird sacred to Woden) and deposited in a white ash tree (likewise associated with the god); because the arm was incorrupt, the tree was endowed with 'ageless vigour'. The raven then dropped the arm to the ground where a spring rose up. The site of the tree became Oswestry 'Oswald's Tree'.[60]

58   Gunton (1686), p. 12.
59   Marilyn Dunn (2009) *The Christianization of the Anglo-Saxons c. 597–c. 700: Discourses of Life, Death and Afterlife*, London: Continuum,, p. 73. On Oswald's deliberate raising of the cross as a Christianisation of the world-tree see p. 112.
60   Gábor Klaniczay (2002) *Holy Rulers and Blessed Princesses: Dynastic Cults in Medieval Central Europe*,

These strikingly pagan motifs suggest, at the very least, the Christianisation of a previously pagan site, but they also seem to assimilate Oswald's identity to Woden himself. Oswald, who may have died as a sacrifice to Woden, becomes in effect a Woden-substitute – a paradox made possible by the fact that, in Norse mythology, Woden hangs himself (as a sacrifice to himself) on the world-tree.

The relic of St Oswald at Peterborough (and the reliquary that enclosed it) was considered so valuable that a special spiral staircase or 'vice' still survives that would have led to a spy hole at which a monk known as the horuspex stood guard over the relic.[61] The last reference to the shrine of St Oswald's arm was in July 1518 when the sacrist of the monastery was accused of stealing jewels from the reliquary and giving them to women in the town.[62] No mention of the arm was made by the commissioners sent by Henry VIII to dissolve the monastery in 1539, and the fate of St Oswald's arm after the Reformation is unknown. Gunton noted that 'Nicolas Harpsfield a late Historical Romanist would make us believe, that the prayer of Aydanus was still in force, as if that arm was somewhere extant'.[63] Gunton was alluding to Nicholas Harpsfield's *Historia Anglicana ecclesiastica* (*English Ecclesiastical History*), published in 1622 but written in the 1570s, in which he claimed that '[Aidan's] prayer has never failed down to these our times'.[64] Harpsfield's words appear to suggest that he knew the location of the arm of St Oswald after 1539, but he offers no clues. In addition to the chapel of St Oswald in the south transept of Peterborough Cathedral, another reminder of the saint's connection to the city is the Roman Catholic church of the Sacred Heart and St Oswald on Lincoln Road.

Gods and monsters: the nave ceiling of Peterborough Minster

One of the greatest glories of Peterborough Minster is the remarkable painted ceiling of the nave completed under Abbot Walter of Bury St Edmunds (ruled 1233–45) for the solemn consecration of the completed church on 6 October 1238. The decorative scheme of the ceiling is complex, and at times baffling. Many attempts have been made to decode and interpret the different figures who appear, framed in the ceiling's distinctive lozenges.[65] What is most noticeable is that many of the figures do

Cambridge: Cambridge University Press, p. 168. On 'pagan' elements in the cult of St Oswald see also David Rollason (1995) 'St Oswald in post-Conquest England' , pp. 164–77 in Claire Stancliffe and Eric Cambridge (eds), *Oswald: Northumbrian King to European Saint,* Stamford: Paul Watkins, at p. 170; Annemiek Jansen (1995) 'The development of the St Oswald legends on the Continent', pp. 230–40 in Stancliffe and Cambridge, at p. 239.

61   Higham (1988), p. 18.
62   Higham (1988), p. 19.
63   Gunton (1686), p. 14.
64   Nicholas Harpsfield (1622) *Historia Anglicana ecclesiastica,* Douai, p. 91: '*cuius precatio ad haec nostra tempora nunquam frustrata est*'.
65   For a history of the interpretation of the ceiling see Jackie Hall and Susan M. Wright (eds) (2015) *Conservation and Discovery: Peterborough Cathedral Nave Ceiling and Related Structures,* London: Museum of London Archaeology, pp. 12–13.

not belong to Christian iconography and some hark to the pagan past, such as the two-faced Roman god Janus.

The first attempt to interpret the ceiling systematically was made by the eighteenth-century amateur antiquary Thomas Pownall (1722–1805), who was governor of the colony of Massachusetts 1757–60 and, even after the American War of Independence, continued to style himself 'Governor Pownall'. Pownall had an intense interest in the development of Gothic architecture, partly derived from his upbringing in Lincoln and partly from his Freemasonry.[66] However, Pownall was also interested in the history of art and painting, and on 6 and 13 March and 3 April 1788 he read portions of a letter on medieval painting to the Society of Antiquaries of London which included detailed analysis of the ceiling of Peterborough Minster. The letter was printed in the Society's proceedings, *Archaeologia*, and included the earliest printed depictions of the ceiling.[67]

Pownall was particularly intrigued by two figures: a monkey sitting backwards on a running goat holding an owl, and the figure of a woman standing in a chariot or waggon. Pownall interpreted the monkey as 'an emblematic figure, characterising the degeneracy and pride of the nobility', noting that the figure is:

carried in full career by lust, in a situation of infamy. This is exhibited by a monkey, the emblem of the human species degenerate, carrying on his paw an owl, in ridicule of the foolish pride of the nobility carrying on their fist a hawk as a mark of the privilege of nobility. This caricature is riding on a goat. The goat, which is the emblem of lust, is running in full career, while the rider sits with his face to the tail, the known settled position of infamy.[68]

There are, however, other possible interpretations of the 'monkey' riding a goat. In his *De nugis curialium* ('Concerning trifles of courtiers'), the medieval author Walter Map (1140–c. 1210) tells the story of a British king, Herla, who is visited by a grotesque, pigmy-sized creature riding a goat, 'hairy like Pan', who proposes that he and his people bring gifts to Herla's forthcoming wedding on condition that Herla visit him in a year's time. After a year Herla is summoned and the hirsute fairy king entertains Herla for three days. When Herla leaves, the king gives him a greyhound to sit in front of his saddle and warns him not to dismount until the greyhound leaps down. When Herla returns to his kingdom he finds that 300 years have passed, and when his companions dismount they crumble to dust; so Herla is still riding, waiting for the greyhound to jump down, and this is the origin of Harlekin's or Harlequin's host, reported to

66   See Thomas Pownall (1788–89a) 'Observations on the origin and progress of Gothic architecture, and on the Corporation of Free Masons supposed to be the establishers of it as a regular order', *Archaeologia*, 9, pp. 110–26.
67   Thomas Pownall (1788–89b) 'Observations on ancient painting in England. In a letter from Gov. Pownall, to the Rev. Michael Lort, D. D. V. P. A. S.', *Archaeologia*, 9, pp. 141–56, engraving of figures from the ceiling on plate facing p. 146.
68   Pownall (1788–89b), p. 147.

Figure 7 A monkey riding backwards on a goat, from the nave ceiling of Peterborough Minster. Engraving from Pownall (1788–89b), plate facing p. 146.

be the host of the dead in the eleventh century by Orderic Vitalis.[69]

Given Peterborough's association with the Wild Hunt, it is tempting to interpret the 'monkey' on the nave ceiling as Map's goat-mounted fairy king. The positions of both monkey and goat resemble medieval depictions of witches flying to the Sabbath, a belief in turn derived from the story of the Wild Hunt.[70] However, it is important not to put too much store in images and stories from different eras and countries. In 1937 C. J. P. Cave and T. Borenius undertook a thorough analysis of the imagery of the ceiling, and noted the similarity between the monkey on a goat on the nave ceiling and a similar figure in the Peterborough Psalter in Brussels, speculating that 'it may have had some magical significance', an impression heightened by the fact that the monkey is apparently blessing the owl.[71] H. W. Janson noted that the goat and owl are both 'devilish creatures associated, respectively, with lechery and paganism', but agreed with Pownall that the image was 'satire at the expense of the nobility'.[72] Folke Nordström drew attention to parallels between the Peterborough monkey on a goat and other medieval representations of the vice of luxury, which often depict a naked woman riding backwards on a goat,[73] an image that later came to be associated in Continental Europe with the wild ride to the witches' Sabbath.

The second image that attracted Pownall's attention was 'a singular emblematic figure … a woman riding in a self-moved cart'. This particular image was drastically repainted in the 1830s and is now barely recognisable as the image reproduced in Pownall's engraving (although it should be noted that the ceiling had previously been

---

69 Briggs (2002), pp. 60–1.

70 Most notably Hans Baldung's 1510 engraving of a witches' Sabbath, which depicts a naked young woman riding backwards on a goat through the air. See metmuseum.org/art/collection/search/336235, accessed 4 December 2016.

71 C. J. P. Cave and T. Borenius (1937) 'The painted ceiling in the nave of Peterborough Cathedral', *Archaeologia*, 88, pp. 297–309, at p. 300.

72 H. W. Janson (1952) *Apes and Ape Lore in the Middle Ages and the Renaissance,* London: Warburg Institute, p. 166.

73 Folke Nordström (1955) 'Peterborough, Lincoln and the science of Robert Grosseteste: a study in thirteenth century architecture and iconography', *Art Bulletin,* 37, pp. 241–72, at p. 246.

Figure 8 The 'harvest dame' from the nave ceiling of Peterborough Minster. Engraving from Pownall (1788–89b), plate facing p. 146.

repainted in the 1740s).[74] Pownall concluded that the woman was a personification of the harvest season:

> As Janus at the East end of the cieling may be supposed to have reference to the commencement of the year, so this figure may be meant to represent the harvest dame, holding the harvest moon in her hand. I observed a peculiarity, that the hand of the woman which carries the moon is muffled in the drapery, the other hand and arm is bare.[75]

Although Nordström describes this figure as nothing more than 'a personification of the moon',[76] and notes that it was heavily altered by repainting in the nineteenth century, Pownall's decision to identify the image as the 'harvest dame' is a reminder of an Anglo-Saxon pagan custom that lingered in medieval England. An agricultural ritual known as the *æcerbot* ('field remedy'), first recorded in the eleventh century, involved the chanting of the words *erce, erce, erce, eorþan modor* ('erce, erce, erce, Earth's Mother').[77] Although it is unclear who 'Earth's Mother' is in this rite, she is clearly a pagan survival and may be identifiable with the Germanic fertility god or goddess Nerthus, who according to Tacitus travelled around the land in a waggon and was identical with, or married to, *Terra Mater* (Mother Earth).[78] Nerthus/Terra Mater was worshipped by the Angli, the first-century ancestors of the English in their original homeland of northern Frisia and southern Denmark.

In September 1598 a German traveller in England, Paul Hentzer, came across a celebration of 'Harvest Home' between Windsor and Eton. The last of the harvest

---

74   Hall and Wright (2015), p. 110.

75   Pownall (1788–89b), pp. 147–8.

76   Nordström (1955), p. 251.

77   Daniel Anlezark (2013) 'The Anglo-Saxon world view', pp. 66–81 in M. Godden and M. Lapidge (eds), *The Cambridge Companion to Old English Literature*, 2nd edn, Cambridge: Cambridge University Press, at pp. 66–7.

78   Richard North (1997) *Heathen Gods in Old English Literature,* Cambridge: Cambridge University Press, pp. 45–7.

was piled onto a decorated cart along with 'an image richly dressed, by which perhaps they would signify Ceres'.[79] It was quite natural that an educated man like Hentzer, steeped in Renaissance Classicism, would have identified the figure as Ceres, and a 'Harvest Queen' riding in a cart at a pageant in honour of Queen Elizabeth at Kenilworth in 1575 was similarly identified as Ceres.[80] However, learned commentators often adopted the Classical tradition of *interpretatio Romana*, exemplified by Julius Caesar who refused to name Gaulish gods and instead identified them with their Roman equivalents. To a learned Renaissance observer, *any* harvest goddess was to be identified with Ceres, and this says nothing about what the people celebrating Harvest Home thought about their image.

Scholars are divided on whether the 'corn dolly' traditionally made from the last sheaf to be harvested represents a diminished version of the 'harvest dame' figure in her cart, or whether Hentzer was describing a separate and distinct tradition.[81] However, Pownall's suggestion that the woman in a cart holding the moon was the 'harvest dame' suggests that the figure strongly reminded him of English harvest customs. Whether those customs were survivals of ancient Germanic paganism is disputed, and we have no evidence for a 'goddess' being drawn around the fields in a cart until the sixteenth century, but Pownall's explanation of the moon in the woman's hand as the harvest moon nevertheless still seems compelling.

Another image, dismissed by Pownall as 'a grotesque fancy figure',[82] was given more attention by Nordström, who interpreted it as a representation of the devil as a pagan deity. The image depicts 'a frightful beast with long, pointed ears, big jaws, and impressive tail, the hind legs of a buck but the arms and hands of a human being'. This devil holds a hammer, 'perhaps a reference to the pagan god Hephaestus', and a banner bearing a swastika, a pagan symbol of the sun. Nordström agreed with Cave and Borenius that the siting of this image next to the Agnus Dei (a depiction of the Lamb of God holding a banner, representing the Resurrection) was significant, but disagreed with them that the devil represents death in contrast to life because the swastika is a pagan symbol of life. He concludes that 'the Devil with the hammer and swastika symbolises the heathen god and thus, of course, everlasting death'.[83]

If Nordström's identification of this figure as the devil in the guise of a pagan god is correct, it raises the question why the monks of Peterborough should have considered it necessary, in the thirteenth century, to contrast Christianity with a paganism long since defeated in England. The hammer wielded by the devil, identified by Nordström with the hammer of the Roman smith-god Hephaestus, might also be linked with the Norse god Thor and his English equivalent Thunor, but there is no convincing evidence of the survival of pagan beliefs in medieval England beyond the tenth century, when the last vestiges of Viking paganism were suppressed. However, English monks had been actively

79   Quoted in Hutton (1996), pp. 333–4.
80   Quoted in Hutton (1996), pp. 333–4.
81   For a full discussion see Hutton (1996), pp. 332–47.
82   Pownall (1788–9b), p. 147.
83   Nordström (1955), p. 244.

involved in the conversion of Scandinavia and the Baltic region before the Norman Conquest, and some abbeys retained their Scandinavian links into the Norman and Plantagenet eras.[84] Efforts to convert the Baltic region continued throughout the Middle Ages, while Lapland remained pagan until the seventeenth century. The choice of images on the painted nave ceiling would suggest that the threat of paganism, and the pagan legacy, continued to exist on the mental horizons of the monks of medieval Peterborough.

Well worship

One of the most visible and obvious ways in which early English Christianity adapted to preexisting pagan beliefs was in the adoption of wells and sacred springs as holy wells, rededicated to saints rather than gods and water spirits. It was common for Christian sites to be established near natural springs and pools fed by them – partly for the practical reason that, at this early period, a water source was needed for multiple baptisms of adults by full immersion. However, springs and bodies of water also played a significant role in Anglo-Saxon pagan beliefs – something we glimpse in the epic poem *Beowulf* (where the antagonist Grendel and his mother live in a sinister mere).[85] The practice of well worship always sat uneasily with the church authorities, who would suppress it if they thought it went too far. The problem was not the veneration of wells in itself – many stories of the saints, including the tale of St Oswald's arm, contained tales of a spring bubbling up miraculously from the ground – but the veneration by the laity of unsanctioned sacred sites.

The old name of Peterborough, Medeshamstede, was supposed to derive from 'Medeswael', an area of the River Nene ascribed miraculous properties.[86] Gunton thought that Medeswael was:

> a deep Pit or Gulf, in the River of Nen ... which ancient Writers of the place affirm to have been of wonderful depth, and so cold in the heat of Summer, that no Swimmer was able to abide the cold thereof; and yet in the Winter it was never known to be frozen: Which Properties are now lost with the Well it self; only Tradition hath preserved a dark memory thereof, adventuring to say, It is a little beneath the Bridge that is now standing.[87]

Gunton's description of Medeswael as miraculously unfrozen in winter suggests that a vague belief in the pool's supernatural properties lingered even in the seventeenth century. The natural historian John Morton, writing in 1712, identified 'Medeswael' as an example of a swallow-hole, 'Inlets of Rain-Water, which having fallen upon the Surface of the

---

84   David Knowles (1963) *The Monastic Order in England*, 2nd edn, Cambridge: Cambridge University Press, pp. 67–9.

85   See George Lyman Kittredge (1928) *Witchcraft in Old and New England*, Cambridge, Mass.: Harvard University Press, pp. 33–4; Hutton (1993) pp. 298–9.

86   See Robert E. Lewis (ed.) (1999) *Middle English Dictionary*, Ann Arbor, Mi.: University of Michigan Press, Part W3, p. 279.

87   Gunton (1686), p. 1.

Figure 9 Remains of the
Infirmary of
Peterborough Abbey,
where St Laurence's
Well was located.
Photograph by the
author.

Higher Ground, runs off them into pretty large Streams in some Places'. However, both Gunton and Morton noted that this feature of the river no longer existed by their time.[88]

Gunton observed that in 1290, Bishop Oliver Sutton of Lincoln (in whose diocese Peterborough was then located) condemned as superstitious the holy well of St Edmund of Abingdon at Oxford and another at *Lincelad* (probably Linslade) in Buckinghamshire.[89] Gunton noted that no trace remained of the holy well of St Laurence next to the Infirmary in the Minster precincts at Peterborough, and suggested that it may have been suppressed by Bishop Sutton at around the same time. The location of St Laurence's well close to the Infirmary (whose chapel was dedicated to St Laurence) makes practical sense, given that an infirmary caring for sick monks required a reliable source of fresh water. However, it is also possible that the Infirmary was built close to the holy well owing to a belief in its healing properties, which seems also to have attracted the interest of lay pilgrims to Peterborough.

Although holy wells served as a substitute for earlier pagan beliefs, it seems that some pagan beliefs about wells did survive in the Fens, at least as late as the eleventh century. In 1071 William the Conqueror, desperate to end the siege of Ely

---

88   Morton (1712), p. 308.

89   Gunton (1686), p. 227. Gunton included the original Latin text of Bishop Sutton's denunciation of the wells at Oxford and Linslade on pp. 341–2.

(where Hereward the Wake was holding out against the Normans), agreed to engage the services of a woman from Brandon with a reputation for witchcraft. However, Hereward heard about the plan, went to Brandon, disguised himself as a peasant and stayed in the same house as the woman. In the middle of the night the woman got up and went to a spring near the house:

> Getting up in the middle of the night, she withdrew to the springs of water, which flowed out nearby in the eastern part of the same house;[90] he followed her secretly when she went out and began to try her incantations. And he heard answers, I do not know of whom, from the guardian of the springs; these I scarcely know. [Hereward] wanted to kill her, but questions unheard delayed him.

The Normans planned to set the woman on a high gantry in order to hurl curses at the English, but because Hereward knew all about the Normans' plan in advance, he arranged for his warriors to creep out of the reeds and set fire to the gantry, which fell and killed the woman. The woman's attempt to communicate with a 'guardian of the springs' is highly suggestive of a surviving pre-Christian belief in water sprites which, if it lingered as late as the eleventh century at Brandon, might also have been alive and well in other areas – and explains why the church authorities were so keen to suppress well worship. However, the suppression of St Laurence's Well may have been down to the fact that it was so close to the Minster, and plenty of other holy wells existed in the area: St Leonard's Well on the western edge of the city, Holywell near Longthorpe, East Well near Helpston and Sacrewell near Thornhaugh (see Chapter 3).

---

90 Another version of the story has 'streams of water flowing out on the east side of the house, next to the garden' (*fontes aquarum in orientem affluentes juxta hortum domus*). See *Gesta Herwardi*, vol. 1, p. 385.

Chapter 2

Magic, miracles and witchcraft

Belief in witchcraft, the devil, miracles and magic was an important feature of Peterborough's past and ever-present in the folklore of the surrounding region. England's earliest recorded case of witchcraft by sticking pins in someone's effigy comes from Ailsworth in the Soke of Peterborough, yet belief in witchcraft was by no means confined to the Middle Ages. In 1601 a witch was executed at Peterborough, and local people remained convinced of the reality of witchcraft as late as the 1950s. Yet witchcraft was only one of several supernatural forces at work in Peterborough's past. Before the Reformation, belief in the miraculous power of relics and other holy things was widespread and approved by the church. Fear of the devil dominated one period in the history of medieval Peterborough Abbey, since he was thought to have cursed the monastery, and a stark warning of the punishment for magicians – a pillar representing the fall of Simon Magus – still stands at the entrance to Peterborough Cathedral. Yet the monks of Peterborough remained interested in magic, judging from the contents of their monastic library.

This chapter explores stories involving the devil in the medieval history of Peterborough Abbey, the magical interests of Peterborough's medieval monks, and the development of the unauthorised Peterborough folk-saint Laurence of Oxford. It also addresses what we know about belief in witchcraft in the Peterborough area. The chapter also examines the possibility that the 'plough witches' who were part of Plough Monday festivities in Peterborough were somehow connected with witchcraft, before dealing with toadmen (a particular kind of male agricultural witch), practices of counter-witchcraft, and belief in witchcraft and magic in modern Peterborough.

The witch of Ailsworth

One of the earliest accounts of witchcraft in English history occurs in a charter of King Edgar that may refer to events that occurred in 948 but was written between 963 and 975. The charter is a grant of lands to a man named Wulfstan Ucca, confirming his ownership of Ailsworth because:

> a widow and her son had previously forfeited the land at Ailsworth because they drove iron pins into Wulfstan's father, Ælfsige. And it was detected and the murderous instrument dragged from her chamber; and the woman was seized, and drowned at London Bridge, and her son escaped and became an outlaw.[1]

---

1   Dorothy Whitelock (ed.) (1953) *English Historical Documents, c. 500–1042*, London: Eyre & Spottiswoode, p. 519.

Most historians interpret this incident as an early case of effigy magic, a type of sorcery found in many cultures that involves sticking pins in an image of someone with the hope that it will cause actual harm to the person. The practice is frequently attested in the later Middle Ages but the Ailsworth example is the only mention of a specific case in Anglo-Saxon England. However, the practice was prohibited in Anglo-Saxon penitentials (books compiled by the church containing lists of sins and the penances prescribed for them).

Not all historians agree that the widow of Ailsworth and her son were engaged in witchcraft. Carole Hough argues that there is no actual mention of an effigy in the original Old English, which says simply 'they drove iron pins into Wulfstan's father' (*hi drifon serne stacan on Ælsie Wulfstanes feder*) and states that a *morð* was dragged from her chamber. The Old English word *morð* (from which we derive 'murder') usually meant 'death' but could also refer to the instrument that caused someone's death. Hough suggests that the passage can just as easily be interpreted as referring to a literal physical assault on Ælfsige by the widow and her son with an iron bar.[2] However, witchcraft is still the most likely interpretation of this passage, since *drifon* ('drove') would be a peculiar word to use for a literal attack on someone with an iron bar. Furthermore, the widow's manner of death suggests that she was the victim of an ordeal by swimming, a standard procedure in Anglo-Saxon England for determining someone's guilt but later particularly associated with detecting witches.

It may be significant that the Ailsworth incident occurred before Bishop Ethelwold of Winchester's re-foundation of the Abbey of Burgh in 970. During the preceding century, following Medeshamstede's complete destruction by the Danes, there was no central organisation of Christianity in the region and the inhabitants may have reverted to paganism or, if they were Danish settlers, simply continued their pagan ancestral customs in a new land. The Peterborough area had a particularly high Danish population in the tenth century, with around a third of its people having Scandinavian names.[3] The names of the widow of Ailsworth and her son are not recorded, but it is conceivable that the unusual appearance of the 'pagan' practice of effigy-based sorcery could be related to the presence of a barely converted Danish population.

Simon Magus

One of the most striking sights for the visitor entering Peterborough Cathedral for the first time is a gruesome scene depicted on the base of the central column dividing the western portal, which was completed by 1193. The column base of dark Purbeck or Alwalton marble depicts a man upside down being tormented by demons. M. R. James, the early twentieth-century Cambridge antiquary better known for his spine-

---

2   Carole Hough (2014) *'An Ald Reht': Essays on Anglo-Saxon Law*, Newcastle-upon-Tyne: Cambridge Scholars Publishing, p. 98; On this case see also A. Davies (1989) 'Witches in Anglo-Saxon England: five case histories', pp. 41–56 in D. G. Scragg (ed.), *Superstition and Popular Medicine in Anglo-Saxon England*, Manchester: Manchester University Press, at pp. 49–51.

3   H. C. Darby (1936) *An Historical Geography of England before A.D. 1800*, Cambridge: Cambridge University Library, p. 148.

Figure 10 Simon Magus carried off by devils, from a column base at the west end of Peterborough Minster. Photograph by the author.

chilling ghost stories, was the first person to identify the scene as the fall of Simon Magus, the biblical character who gave his name to the sin of simony (attempting to buy or sell grace).[4] In the Acts of the Apostles (8: 9–24) Simon is a magician who converts to Christianity but then offers the apostles money to be able to lay hands on someone and impart the Holy Spirit. However, later tradition inflated Simon's verbal exchange with Peter in Acts into a full-blown magical contest between the apostle's miraculous powers and Simon's false magic.

The version represented at Peterborough seems to be derived from the apocryphal *Acts of Peter and Paul*, in which Peter, Paul and Simon appear before the Emperor Nero to test their powers. Simon levitates from a high wooden tower but owing to the prayers of Peter and Paul he falls to his death where his body is divided into four parts; the devils on the Peterborough column, each one of whom has seized an arm or leg, appear to be tearing Simon's body into quarters. Both M. R. James and George Henderson noted that the column base was supposed to contrast Simon's downfall with Peter's exaltation in the tympanum of the west front above (no longer visible because the Galilee porch was built over it). The image was an invocation of the Abbey's apostolic protection as well as an implied threat against anyone who tried to challenge its privileges.[5] The image of Simon Magus at

---

4   M. R. James (1894–98) 'On the paintings formerly in the Choir at Peterborough', *Proceedings of the Cambridge Antiquarian Society,* 9, pp. 178–94. See also Alberto Ferreiro (2005) *Simon Magus in Patristic, Medieval and Early Modern Traditions*, Leiden, Netherlands: Brill, p. 326. Ferreiro pp. 307–36 comprehensively surveys all representations of Simon Magus in western art.

5   George Henderson (1981) 'The damnation of Nero and related themes', pp. 39–51 in A. Borg and A.

the entrance of the abbey church served simultaneously as a warning against simony, sorcery and any kind of presumption, as well as being a reminder of the power of St Peter and the trickery of demons; demons had helped Simon to fly but subsequently turned on him to punish him for his misdeeds.[6]

Speak of the Devil

In spite of the dramatic warning against trafficking with demons placed at the very entrance to the abbey church, the monks of Peterborough did not always manage to stay away from trouble with the devil. In 1041 Æthelric, a monk of Peterborough, was chosen as bishop of Durham. Æthelric began to replace the church at Chester-le-Street with a new one, and during the process of knocking down the old church he discovered a large quantity of treasure. In the Middle Ages (and indeed long afterwards) it was widely believed that treasure was guarded by evil spirits who would take revenge on those who removed it.[7] However, Bishop Æthelric did not just remove the treasure but also sent much of it to his home monastery of Peterborough. In doing so, he was in breach of church law because Chester-le-Street lay within the Diocese of Durham and its treasure belonged to Durham.

Æthelric was forced to resign over the treasure scandal in 1056, and returned to Peterborough, but he had inadvertently brought a curse on the monastery by meddling with the buried treasure, as Gunton recounts:

> In the time of Abbot Leofricus his sickness, this Egelricus being at his accustomed Evening devotions, the Devil appeared to him, in the shape of a boy of terrible countenance, and told him, that ere long he should triumph over the chiefest of them (which perhaps was in the death of Leofricus Abbot) and that three several times he would revenge himself upon the Monks, and Monastery, telling him also the manner. First, that he would cause all the Monks to be expelled, and the goods of the Monastery to be taken away. Secondly, he would cause the Monastery to be set on fire. Thirdly, he would set the Monks so at strife, that they should cut one anothers throats. But Egelricus replying, The Lord rebuke thee, Satan; the Devil vanished, and left a horrible stink behind him.[8]

During the abbacy of John de Séez (1114–25) the second part of the curse laid on the Abbey by the devil came to pass, when a great fire caused huge damage in 1116. According to the chronicler Hugh Candidus, this was because the Abbot and a servant in the monastery inadvertently invoked the devil:

Martindale (eds), *The Vanishing Past: Studies in Medieval Art, Liturgy and Metrology presented to Christopher Hohler*, Oxford: Oxford University Press.

6   The monks' interest in Simon Magus continued, judging from the fact that the monastic library contained a book entitled *Altercatio apostolorum cum Simone Mago* ('The altercation of the apostles with Simon Magus') in the fourteenth century (Gunton (1686), p. 179).

7   On medieval beliefs about buried treasure see Johannes Dillinger (2012) *Magical Treasure Hunting in Europe and North America: A History*, London: Palgrave Macmillan, pp. 28–52.

8   Gunton (1686), p. 16.

The abbot, on the same day, had cursed the house, and on account of anger; and since he was very angry he too unwarily committed it to the enemy. For the fathers had come into the refectory in the morning to lay the tables and displeased him, and he cursed them and at once left to hear a plea at Castor. But a certain man serving for the first time, when we was making fire and it did immediately blaze up said angrily, 'Come, Devil, and blow on the fire'; and at once the fire blazed up, and reached as far as the roof.[9]

The actions of Abbot John were hardly necromancy (deliberate summoning of the devil), but the story is a reminder of how seriously medieval people took even a casual and inadvertent curse, which might invoke the devil and bring disaster, as well as the potentially awful consequences of appropriating buried treasure. In this case, the curse resulted in the building of the present church to replace its Anglo-Saxon predecessor.

Magic in the Peterborough Lapidary

Many of the books in a medieval monastic library would have contained what, to modern eyes, would appear to be magic. Reports of the marvellous and the inexplicable, especially those found in Classical authors, were often accepted as true without much critical analysis.

One surviving book that may have belonged to the monastic library of Peterborough Abbey is a collection of *materia medica* (medical materials), including the longest medieval English treatise on the properties of stones and minerals, known as the Peterborough Lapidary.[10] Composed in the late fifteenth century, the Peterborough Lapidary is an encyclopaedia of 145 stones, many of which are ascribed overtly magical properties. Although the practice of magic was forbidden by the church, the Peterborough Lapidary does nothing to censure it. It suggests that some stones will protect the bearer against harmful magic. Capnite 'will defend ... from wicked enchantments',[11] yet magicians' use of magnets is presented as a recommendation of their effectiveness: '[Telemus] the enchanter used it much, for he knew well that it helped much for enchantments; and after him the marvellous enchanter Circe, who was a woman, used it much'.[12] Likewise, 'a magus' (or possibly *the* Simon Magus) is given as the authority for the claim that the stone adredamia 'may be able to settle willing minds'.[13]

---

9   Quoted in Thomas Craddock (1864) *Peterborough Cathedral: A General, Architectural, and Monastic History*, Peterborough: J. S. Clarke, p. 40: *Abbas enim eadem die maledixerat domum, et per iram, quia iracundus erat nimis commendavit incaute inimico. Intraverant autem patres mane refectorium, ut emendarent tabulas, et displicuit ei, et maledixit, et statim exivit ad placitum apud Castre. Sed et quidam serviens de pristino cum faceret ignem et non cito arderet iratus dixit; veni Diabole et insuffla ignem; et statim ignis arsit; et usque ad tectum pervenit.*

10   For a discussion of the provenance of the Peterborough Lapidary see Francis Young (ed.) (2016a) *A Medieval Book of Magical Stones: The Peterborough Lapidary*, Cambridge: Texts in Early Modern Magic, pp. xx–xxiv.

11   Young (2016a), p. 27.

12   Young (2016a), p. 62.

13   Young (2016a), p. 13.

The Peterborough Lapidary is also ambivalent towards witchcraft. The Lapidary contains advice on counter-witchcraft, yet at the same time the practice of witches is appealed to as an authority for the occult properties of some stones. We are told that witches use a kind of agate to 'change tempests and dry up rivers and streams, as it is said',[14] and 'witches' are given as the authority for the claim that pyrite 'refines hastiness and wrath of hearts'.[15] We are told of magnets that 'witches use this stone very much'.[16] Witches are likewise the authority for coral's resistance to lightning.[17] Bloodstone, on the other hand, has a role to play in counter-witchcraft, since the stone 'discerns the folly of enchantments, and of witches who enjoy the pride of their own wonders, by which they beguile men with the wonders they work'.[18] Likewise, jet 'prevents witchcraft and charms',[19] while sardine 'preserves his bearer from enchantments and from witchcraft'.[20] Sapphire seems to act both against and for witches: 'the sapphire is very good … to break witchcraft', yet 'witches love this stone especially well, for they believe that they do certain wonders by the virtue of this stone'.[21]

In addition to its ambivalence towards witchcraft, the Peterborough Lapidary fails to condemn the use of stones for necromancy (commerce with the devil or the souls of the dead). Instead, the Lapidary presents the use of stones by necromancers as a recommendation: 'Those who use necromancy say that they are more able to have answer of God and are more heard by the sapphire than by other precious stones'.[22] Onyx 'allows a man to speak to his dead friend by night in a meeting',[23] while diadochus makes a dead body move, 'And if you want, you may command whichever devil of hell you want and the devil will do no man harm'.[24] Likewise, the bearer of anancite 'may command the devil to you, and he will obey you whatever you want to say, and he will do you no harm'.[25]

The Peterborough Lapidary also betrays the influence of astrological magic (magic based on drawing down the influences of the stars) by insisting that certain stones must be set in a specific metal in order to enable or enhance their effectiveness. According to astrological magical theory, herbs, stones and metals corresponded with different planetary influences; combining them (by setting a stone under one planet in a metal under another, for example) allowed the astral magician to manipulate heavenly forces on earth. So, for instance, diamond, toadstone, jacinth, topaz and ruby must

14   Young (2016a), p. 4.
15   Young (2016a), p. 15.
16   Young (2016a), p. 63.
17   Young (2016a), p. 25.
18   Young (2016a), p. 41.
19   Young (2016a), p. 47.
20   Young (2016a), p. 71.
21   Young (2016a), p. 65.
22   Young (2016a), p. 67.
23   Young (2016a), p. 90.
24   Young (2016a), p. 37.
25   Young (2016a), p. 13.

be set in gold. Both jasper and onyx are said to have greater virtue when set in gold.[26] Serpentine, on the other hand, may be set in either gold or silver.[27]

Sympathetic magic – the idea that physical resemblance enables magical effectiveness – also features in the Peterborough Lapidary. It is because toadstone, found in the head of the venomous toad, contains a shape like a toad that it is effective as a remedy against poison and venom: 'sometimes the shape of the toad seems to be within it, with broad and shaped feet'.[28]

The Peterborough Lapidary not only condones but also enables the conjuration of demons; indeed, it even includes ritual prescriptions of its own. Whoever wants to engrave jasper should do so 'with a sword in his hand, with a stole about his neck and a staff that should be of olive wood'.[29] Sword, stole and rod are the standard tools of the ritual magician, signifying authority over spirits. The requirement for the engraver of jasper to be equipped as a ritual magician implies either that the stone was protected by spirits or that engraving the stone was meant to call spirits into it, thereby turning the stone into a magical talisman. The Lapidary also claims that celidony, a stone supposedly found in the womb of a swallow, 'is very valuable if it is held up at the sacrament and is wound in a linen cloth'.[30] This is a reference to the elevation or 'sacring', the moment in the mass when the consecrated host was lifted up and shown to the people. White linen was associated with purity in books of ritual magic, and the consecration of celidony resembles the consecrations of *lamina* (pieces of metal inscribed with magical sigils) in texts of necromancy.[31]

The Peterborough Lapidary's insistence on the connection between the powers of stones and the spiritual state of their owners also takes it into magical territory. Ritual magicians, like exorcists, believed that the effectiveness of their operations depended on their personal purity and freedom from sin: the sacraments of the church worked automatically (*ex opere operato*) but exorcism and magic worked *ex opere operantis* – 'from the deed of the operator'. The Peterborough Lapidary suggests that, while the power of stones is inherent in their nature, because it derives from God and is holy it can also be diminished by the sins of the bearer. Being out of mortal sin is given as a condition for bearing several stones, and 'He who bears sardine, onyx and chalcedony will be well enriched, unless he loses his virtue through sin'.[32]

The Lapidary even offers a solution for 're-charging' stones that have lost their virtue on account of sin: 'if any stone has lost his virtue through sin, let a man confess his sin, and take and wash the crystal in pure water and touch the stone with [crystal], and soon he will take his virtue again by the virtue of the crystal'.[33]

---

26   Young (2016a), pp. 53, 89–90.
27   Young (2016a), p. 61.
28   Young (2016a), p. 89.
29   Young (2016a), p. 53.
30   Young (2016a), p. 24.
31   See Paul Foreman (2015) *The Cambridge Book of Magic: A Tudor Necromancer's Manual,* ed. F. Young, Cambridge: Texts in Early Modern Magic, pp. 3, 34, 40, 65, 68, 84, 102, 114.
32   Young (2016a), p. 20.
33   Young (2016a), p. 22.

The Peterborough Lapidary also includes stones with properties enabling divination. If someone 'washes his mouth and holds [a sapphire] under his tongue, as long as the moon is waxing, a man may divine from the morning until midday'.[34] Similarly, 'If a man puts [calonite] in his mouth early in the morning until the sixth hour of the waxing of the moon, he may divine all that is to come after'.[35] Emerald is likewise recommended for divination, and the Lapidary recounts the story that the Emperor Nero had an emerald mirror in which he saw 'all that he sought or desired'.[36] Magical mirrors were staples of medieval necromancy. The Peterborough Lapidary, although not an avowedly magical text, was a book that would have enabled Peterborough monks to pursue magical interests if they had been so inclined.

A Peterborough folk saint

In the Middle Ages the church's procedures for canonisation were less formal than they are today, and saints would often be created 'by acclamation', meaning that ordinary people considered a dead person a saint and claimed to receive cures at that person's grave site. Attempts to turn people into saints by popular acclamation were particularly common in England; the folk saint Sir John Schorne, a thirteenth-century Buckinghamshire priest who was supposed to have confined the devil in a boot, endured until the Reformation, despite the fact that Schorne had never been formally canonised by Rome. Similarly, attempts were made to start cults of the rebels Simon de Montfort and Thomas of Lancaster as popular martyrs.[37] In 1313 Peterborough gained a popular saint of its own: Laurence of Oxford, chamberlain to the Abbot of Peterborough, Godfrey of Crowland. Laurence was executed in that year for stealing from his master.

Earlier in the year, it had been rumoured that Abbot Godfrey had 'carnal knowledge' of four women in the town, one of whom was Agnes Dochild, the wife of his chamberlain Laurence; the Abbot was also accused of committing sodomy with Laurence himself. The alleged offences were reported to the Bishop of Lincoln, John Dalderby, who cleared Godfrey of the charges on 23 February.[38] However, in April Laurence was indicted by the Abbot's court, accused of stealing tableware and money from the manor of Eye to the value of twelve pounds. In spite of being tried alongside fourteen other alleged accomplices, Laurence alone was found guilty and hanged. He was buried next to the chapel of St Thomas Becket, whose chancel still survives and whose nave originally projected out into the market place where Starbucks now stands.[39]

34 Young (2016a), p. 13.
35 Young (2016a), p. 30.
36 Young (2016a), p. 38.
37 Laura Wertheimer (2006) 'Clerical dissent, popular piety, and sanctity in fourteenth-century Peterborough: the cult of Laurence of Oxford', *Journal of British Studies,* 45, pp. 3–25, at p. 15.
38 Wertheimer (2006), pp. 8–9.
39 Wertheimer (2006), pp. 9–10.

In May Bishop Dalderby attended a meeting of the Abbey's chapter at which further accusations were levelled at Godfrey of Crowland, including engineering the death of Laurence and giving Laurence's wife gifts of dresses. Godfrey managed to clear his reputation again in the bishop's eyes, but by June people had started visiting Laurence's grave site on unofficial pilgrimages. This was encouraged by two of the monks, William of Walton and Geoffrey of Wardington, presumably as a means of defying Abbot Godfrey. Other culprits were priests of the town; Stephen Cobbe, Hugh of Thirlby and Richard of Wansford, the vicar of the church of St John the Baptist, were sentenced to public penance by the bishop of Lincoln in August 1313 for encouraging people to gather at Laurence's grave.[40] On 4 November the priests Cobbe, Thurlby and Wansford were sentenced to stand in the middle of St John's church for three successive Sundays after Epiphany 1314 holding crucifixes above their heads and proclaiming their errors. A layman named John Cook was to stand in the marketplace, stripped of his tunic and holding a crucifix while being whipped with a switch. In addition, all four men were compelled to make an annual pilgrimage to Lincoln for the next seven years.[41]

The cult of Laurence of Oxford seems to have lasted for less than a year, since the punishment of the clergy who had supported it removed any vestige of official support. The vicar of St John's support for the cult strongly suggests that the *cause célèbre* of Laurence the chamberlain became a focus for the conflict between town and abbey, which existed in many medieval towns dominated by large Benedictine abbeys that stifled the town's economic and political development. However, the cult also 'deviated from the medieval church's concept of sanctity', since Laurence had not been distinguished by his holy life, and Laura Wertheimer suggests it may have represented 'a unique or unknown form of sanctity'.[42] It may have reflected 'a near-autonomous, lay continuation of an ancient type of Christianity that endured long after the institutional church had transformed sanctity'.[43] However, the cult of Laurence of Oxford at Peterborough was highly unusual in being encouraged by local clergy.[44] The fact that no one was officially supporting the cult after 1313 need not mean that it fizzled out completely, and it is possible that it continued quietly as a lay phenomenon for some time thereafter.

Witches in Peterborough

In the sixteenth century Peterborough and its surrounding Soke was a separate judicial jurisdiction with its own courts and judges, the so-called Liberty of Peterborough.[45] Before the Reformation, the Liberty was ruled by the abbot of Peterborough and the judges were appointed by him; in 1541, when Peterborough Abbey was erected as a cathedral church by royal charter of Henry VIII, control of the Liberty passed to the

---

40   Wertheimer (2006), pp. 17–18.
41   Wertheimer (2006), p. 21.
42   Wertheimer (2006), p. 13–14.
43   Wertheimer (2006), p. 16.
44   Wertheimer (2006), p. 19.
45   See L. G. (1901) 'The Liberty of Peterborough', *Fenland Notes and Queries*, 5, pp. 355–60.

bishops of Peterborough, and later Lord Burghley. However, the bishop of Peterborough also had jurisdiction over a different kind of court – ecclesiastical courts – in the Soke of Peterborough and the entire Diocese of Peterborough (the county of Northamptonshire).

Church courts were different from civil courts in both the nature of the crimes they tried and the penalties they could hand down. The church courts could put people on trial for blasphemy (including swearing), adultery, fornication (premarital sex) and failure to attend church as well as dabbling in magic and witchcraft. However, the church courts could only impose penances (essentially a form of public shaming), and the most severe sentence they could hand down was excommunication,[46] which meant that a person was barred from attending church and, in theory, all Christians were forbidden to speak to or do business with that person until the excommunication was lifted.

Before 1542 witchcraft was not a criminal offence, merely an ecclesiastical one, which meant that it was not possible for anyone to be executed for witchcraft except in exceptional cases where a person was suspected of treason against the king. Then, between 1542 and 1547, during the last years of the reign of Henry VIII, witchcraft became a crime punishable by death for the first time. Between 1547 and 1563 witchcraft was once again under the jurisdiction of the church courts, but Parliament passed an act in 1563 that made witchcraft a criminal offence once more, and it remained so until 1736. Because witchcraft was a felony, judges were obliged to sentence to death anyone found guilty of this crime. In England, the penalty for witchcraft was death by hanging; only in cases where a witch was found guilty of killing her husband or master (if she was a servant) would she be burned to death.

Most English witchcraft trials revolved around the idea that a marginalised member of a community – usually, but not always, an old woman – had cursed another person (or their children or animals) out of envy or spite, leading to sickness and sometimes death. 'Proof' of witchcraft might include a witness reporting that such a curse had been overheard, a confession from the witch herself (extracted by what today would be considered torture), or the discovery of a 'witch's mark' (an unusual teat or area of insensitive skin) somewhere on the witch's body. This was because witches would sometimes confess to making a pact with an evil spirit in the form of an animal (an imp or familiar) which would come to suck her blood before being sent out to do her evil bidding.

There is only one surviving record of a trial for witchcraft in Peterborough itself, which would have taken place at the Quarter Sessions for the Liberty of Peterborough held in the King's Lodging in the minster precincts. No record of the trial survives, but the parish register of the church of St John the Baptist (which then covered the entire city) records the burial of 'Agnes garret condemned & hanged for a witch' on 15 January 1601.[47] Agnes's execution probably took place at Fengate, where most

---

46   In the unique case of heresy the church courts could hand someone over to be executed by the state.

47   'Parish Registers of St. John the Baptist, Peterborough and Holy Cross Westgate, Canterbury', *The Reliquary*, 26 (October 1885), pp. 83–5, at p. 84. The record is dated 1600, but according to the Julian Calendar followed in England at the time, the year 1600 ran from 25 March 1600–24 March 1601. See

public hangings were conducted, and she would have been buried immediately after-wards. Many people resented the burial of convicted witches in consecrated ground, and several Cambridgeshire witches were buried at the crossroads.[48]

Not everyone, however, was prepared to believe that people accused of witchcraft should be punished. William Piers (1580–1670), bishop of Peterborough 1630–32, attempted to save a woman accused of witchcraft in Staffordshire in 1637,[49] and it is possible that the reluctance of Bishop Piers and his predecessor Thomas Dove (1555–1630) to countenance accusations of witchcraft prevented any trials of people from the Liberty of Peterborough, under the direct temporal and spiritual jurisdiction of the bishop. Dove was not consecrated bishop of Peterborough until 26 April 1601,[50] and the see was vacant at the time of Agnes Garret's trial in January. It is conceivable that local authorities took advantage of the absence of a bishop to settle a score with Agnes Garret.

Bishops such as Dove and Piers were not opposed to witchcraft prosecutions because they did not believe in the reality of witchcraft, but because they knew that witch-craft belief was intimately tied up with the potentially dangerous Puritan movement. Puritans wanted the 'purification' of the Church of England by the removal of any remaining hangovers from the medieval church – including bishops – and many Puritans believed themselves to be under direct attack from the devil, via witches, on account of their 'godliness'.

A famous case that greatly contributed to Puritan interest in witchcraft was the bewitchment of the Throckmorton family of Warboys in Huntingdonshire in 1589–93,[51] and Northamptonshire was likewise a hotbed of Puritan witch-mongering. A major witch panic swept the county in 1612, with women arrested as Yelvertoft, Stanwick, Raunds and Thrapston, which Peter Elmer has argued was in part a reaction against the anti-Puritan policies of Bishop Dove.[52] Dove may have been able to keep witchcraft allegations out of Peterborough itself but he could not stamp out Puri-tanism in his entire diocese.

A later dean (and subsequently bishop) of Peterborough, White Kennett, made strenuous efforts to discredit belief in witchcraft in the eighteenth century, preaching in 1715 that 'Witchcraft … is all but impudent Pretence and Delusion only; a perfect Cheat and Imposition upon the credulous Part of Mankind.'[53] Mark Knights has interpreted Kennett's sermon as an attack on the high church clergy and laity who

also 'A witch at Peterborough', *Journal of the Northamptonshire Natural History Society and Field Club*, 22 (1925), p. 224.

48   Porter (1969), pp. 161, 163.

49   Reginald Trevor Davies (1947) *Four Centuries of Witch Beliefs, with special reference to the Great Rebellion*, London: Methuen, p. 80.

50   Kenneth Fincham, 'Dove, Thomas (1555–1630), bishop of Peterborough', *ODNB*, vol. 16, pp. 757–8.

51   On the Warboys case see Philip C. Almond (2008) *The Witches of Warboys: An Extraordinary Story of Sorcery, Sadism and Satanic Possession*. London: I. B. Tauris.

52   Peter Elmer (2016) *Witchcraft, Witch-hunting and Politics in Early Modern England*, Oxford: Oxford University Press, p. 66.

53   Quoted in Tracy Borman (2013) *Witches: A Tale of Sorcery, Scandal and Seduction*, London: Jonathan Cape, p. 238.

had supported the trial of Jane Wenham, one of the last women in England accused of witchcraft, in 1712.[54]

However, in spite of the rejection of belief in witchcraft by elite figures such as Bishop White, most ordinary people remained convinced that witchcraft was real until well into the nineteenth and twentieth centuries. John Clare recalled two neighbours in Helpston who believed in witchcraft; John Billings the elder 'had a very haunted mind for such things',[55] while George Cousins 'believd in witches and often whisperd his suspicions of suspected neighbours in the Village'.[56] One of Clare's favourite spots in the fields near Helpston was even destroyed owing to suspicions of witchcraft:

> [U]nder an old Ivied Oak in Oxey wood ... I twisted a sallow stoven into an harbour [*sic.* for 'arbour'] which grew into the crampd way in which I had made it ... the old ivied tree was cut down when the wood was cut down and my bower was destroyd[;] the woodmen fancied it a resort for robbers & some thought the crampd way in which the things grew were witch knotts[57] and that the spot was a haunt were witches met.[58]

The idea that places in the locality were meeting places for witches occurs again in Clare's poem 'The sorrows of love', written between 1821 and 1824, in which an old woman recalls visiting a fortune teller, reputedly a witch, with her friend Sally Grey:

> Witches of every shape, that used to meet
> To count the stars, or mutter'd charms repeat.
> Woodmen, in winter, as they pass'd the road,
> Have vow'd they've seen some crawling like a toad;
> And some like owlets veering overhead,
> Shrieking enough to fright the very dead.[59]

Clare, however, dismisses the idea that the fortune-teller was in possession of 'ill-got knowledge of the sky' and portrays her as someone who simply recognised the constellations by their shapes: 'She might know these, which, if 'tis sin to know, / Then everybody is a witch below.'[60] J. B. Smith noted that folkloric evidence from Germany shows that counting stars was a common practice of divination, by no means confined to witches, although English folklore portrayed the practice as dangerous and unlucky. Sarah Houghton-Walker has noted that, although historians tend to portray witches

54   Mark Knights (2011) *The Devil in Disguise: Deception, Delusion and Fanaticism in the Early English Enlightenment*, Oxford: Oxford University Press, p. 214.

55   John Clare (2002) *John Clare by Himself*, ed. E. Robinson and D. Powell, 2nd edn, New York: Routledge, p. 52.

56   Clare (2002) p. 75.

57   Witches were commonly thought to 'bind' people or animals by tying magical knots, usually in string or ribbon but in this case in ivy.

58   Clare (2002), p. 41.

59   Quoted in J. B. Smith (1990) 'John Clare's constellations', *Journal of the John Clare Society*, 9, pp. 5–13, at p. 5.

60   Smith (1990), p. 6.

as 'a malevolent village presence' this is not what Clare's poetry suggests.[61] Unlike educated contemporaries who dismissed supernatural belief as useless or even harmful 'superstition', Clare (although he still uses the word 'superstition') portrays such beliefs as harmless or even beneficial, creating an 'impression of the harmonious coexistence of orthodox and unorthodox elements of the world', including gypsy fortune-telling.[62] On the other hand, Clare seems to have interpreted his mental illness as being under the influence of 'evil spirits – of witch-craft', if a letter of Eliza of 10 August 1831 reproaching him for this belief is accurate.[63]

One local witch lived at Castor and was described by John Hales, an elderly local man who delivered a lecture on his reminiscences at Castor infant school on 28 April 1883:

> Up to the year 1834 there was living in the village a reputed witch. She died at the age of 82 years. So you may fancy her antiquated appearance; nose and chin nearly meeting and walking with a hooked stick. Whether she had the proverbial black cat I am not able to say but this I do know that we boys of that period treated her with very great respect when and wherever we met her. It was generally believed and currently reported that if certain of the farmers killed a pig and did not send her a fry, the pig would not take the sale; If a cow calved and she did not receive what was usual to send on such occasions, the calf would not do well, and when they brewed their ale and forgot to send her new beer the beer would not keep.[64]

The witch described by Hales would have been born in 1752. His account is interesting insofar as it suggests that the old woman's reputation as a witch led her to be respected; most stories of suspected witchcraft from this period concern violence done to the suspect, and up to the late nineteenth century witch swimmings, house burnings and assaults were regularly reported in local newspapers.

Plough witches

One kind of 'witch' that was treated more light-heartedly in Peterborough was the 'plough witches' who appeared in the city on Plough Monday, the first Monday after Epiphany (6 January), when men with blackened faces would pull a plough around the streets.[65] The most detailed account of plough witches in the Peterborough area was provided by John Clare in 1825:

> [I]t is the custom for the plough boys ... to meet at the blacksmiths shop to dress themselves & get ready not with white shirts & ribons but to black their faces with a mixture of soot & greese[,] & [those] that will not undergo this are reckond unworthy

61   Sarah Houghton-Walker (2009) *John Clare's Religion*, Farnham: Ashgate, p. 66.
62   Houghton-Walker (2009), p. 81.
63   Emma Trehane (2005) '"Emma and Johnny": the friendship between Eliza Emmerson and John Clare', *Journal of the John Clare Society*, 24, pp. 69–77, at p. 76.
64   CAMUS (2004), p. 349.
65   Dack (1911), p. 8.

of the [sport] & excluded the company — they get an old skeleton of a plough with out share or colter & attach it to a waggon rope in [which] sticks are crossd & on each side these sticks the boys take their station … they are calld plough bullocks[;] the stoutest [among] them is selected for the holder of the plough & thus equ[ipped] they pull it round the village from door to door for [what] they can get[;] when they have gotten beer at the door they have run the 'wind up' as they [call] it to please their benefactors[,] & chusing the dirtiest place in [the] yard he that gets the most mauled & complains of it the least is reckoned a brave fellow[.] in this wind up they try to entangle the holder of the plough in the ropes who by superior strength not only keeps from tumbling but contrives by dextrously [heaving] & throwing the plough to get most of the plough bullock[s wound] up in their own … to those that will not give [to] them they let loose their mischief by pulling up shoe scrapers at the door or gate posts & winding up the person in the rope & as it is reckoned a lawless day the constable [will] rarely interfere if calld upon – several of the boys of the neigh[bouring] villages used to meet at Milton Hall to get beer [where] they had it without stint when before the wind up commenced [the] different villagers used to bang each others ploughs together & pull against them to try which was the strongest – which cau[sed] such confusion of quareling that it was abolished – the … men grown servants 3 or 4 of them go round the Village dres[sed] up in a grotesque manner[;] they are calld the 'plough witches' 2 of them has their faces blackd & a hunch back of straw [stuck] into their smock frocks[;] their hats are tyd up into a three cockd [form] & figured with chalk[;] in their hands they carry a beesom [&] a spoon filld with soot & greese to sweep the dirt or [to] black the faces of the servants maids they happen to meet with who generally take care to keep out of the way[.] the 'she [witch'] as he is calld is dressd up in a laughable joanish man[ner] in womens cloaths he has no hunch back & his face is ruddled [i.e. painted red][;] they carry a box with half pence in it which they shake [when] they come to the door – at night the bullocks & witches meet together in a sociable party & buying their supper [of] cake & ale.[66]

Clare's account of the Peterborough custom makes clear that (at least in the 1820s) the 'plough bullocks' and 'plough witches' paraded around as separate groups and only met together in the evening; furthermore, there were two kinds of 'plough witch' – ordinary plough witches who blacked their faces like the plough bullocks, and the 'she witch' whose face was painted red. Charles Dack reported that Plough Monday was still celebrated in Peterborough in the 1890s, but implied that by this date the full performance was no longer practised and plough boys simply asked for presents:

On this day gangs of plough-boys still come into Peterborough, and call on the different tradesmen with whom their masters deal, to ask for presents. These gangs of six or more were headed by a man. One boy was dressed as a woman, but all had their faces daubed with soot and red ochre, and dragged an old plough with a wooden share. In the country, if refused a present, the boys were yoked to the plough, and the path in front of the house ploughed up. In the town, the toe of the share was inserted under the scraper, and the plough boys tugged, and away went to scraper. They were called

---

66   Quoted in Deacon (1983), pp. 287–8.

plough witches and Mumpers. The leader used to repeat some doggerel, but I can only remember one verse, and unfortunately I have not been able to find anyone who can remember more. It was:–

> Look ye here and look ye there,
> And look ye over yander,
> And there you'll see the old grey goose
> A-smiling at the gander.[67]

Dack's account bears out Clare's report that the plough witches used to tear up people's boot scrapers, and the boy dressed as a woman corresponds to Clare's 'she witch', but Dack knows of no distinction between the plough bullocks and plough witches as described by Clare, and it is probable that the performance evolved over time between the 1820s and the middle of the nineteenth century, which was presumably the time recalled by Dack's informants. Thomas Davidson thought the 'plough witches' of Northamptonshire and 'plough witchers' of Huntingdonshire were originally a reminder of (or possibly a protection against) the power regularly ascribed to witches of being able to stop a plough by charming the horses.[68] However, blackened faces and cross-dressing were also part of the Huntingdonshire and Fenland tradition of molly dancing, and it could be that the plough witches arose from this, or that the customs were a remnant of a very debased form of drama, now lost, that had been performed on Plough Monday and featured witches as characters. The custom of calling boys dressed as old women 'witches' may have been nothing but humour. On the other hand, it is also possible that the plough witches were a dramatic representation of a specific kind of witch, toadmen.

Toadmen

A particular category of witchcraft in the Fens that was – unusually – specific to men allowed a horseman to gain supernatural powers of control over horses and other animals. A 'toadman' or 'tudman' was a horseman who had obtained a specific bone of a toad in a ritual that was thought to involve making a pact with the devil.[69] Provided the toadman carried the toadbone amulet on him, it gave him the power to pacify or send any horse wild at will.

This characteristic belief of the Fens was particularly enduring in the Peterborough area; in 1953 the folklorist G. W. Pattison reported that the belief had died out around Ely but was still remembered 'and even still held' around Peterborough. Informants from March and Thornhaugh, who had heard stories of toadmen from relatives in Thorney, Eye, Stamford and Wansworth, told Pattison that 'No door is ever closed

---

67   Dack (1899), pp. 323–4.
68   Thomas Davidson (1956–7) 'The horseman's word: a rural initiation ceremony', *Gwerin: A Half-Yearly Journal of Folklore*, 1, pp. 67–74, at p. 71. In 1532 a Colchester smith's wife was accused of witchcraft for charming ploughs to ensure good luck in ploughing (Keith Thomas (1991) *Religion and the Decline of Magic*, 2nd edn, Penguin: Harmondsworth, p. 776).
69   For an account of toadmen in Cambridgeshire see Porter (1969), pp. 55–7.

to a toadman', and that toadmen had faced no problems with rationing of pig-feed during the Second World War, presumably because they could use their powers to keep animals under control.

Pattison reported that, at an adult education class at which toadmen were discussed:

> There was some argument as to whether particular men did not do this by drugs, either bought or home made, from common plants, but the argument was particular, and there was no agreement that this rational explanation covered all cases. The informant who had worked with a toadman often asked him how he did it. The answer was always the same. 'I daren't tell my own son. What I know goes to the churchyard with me'. Another man said that his father had announced his intention of becoming a toadman, whereupon his father (my informant's grandfather) threatened that if he did he would shoot him. The idea was abandoned.[70]

The attitude of Pattison's informants was typical of rural belief in witchcraft in the Fens in the twentieth century; most people understood that their belief did not tally with rationality, but they were nevertheless unwilling to discredit stories they had been told by trustworthy people about rationally inexplicable events. Pattison noted that his informants 'are unable to say they do not believe it, although … they agree that it is of no use with tractors and machinery'.[71]

The ritual for becoming a toadman reported to Pattison was as follows:

> To become a toadman, catch a 'walking toad'. You may then skin it alive if you know how to, or you may peg it to an ant-heap and let the ants eat the bones clean. Toads may be plank-hanged. That's to say that they are stretched out on the end of a plank which is balanced on a crosspiece. The hangman then bangs the other end with a mallet. The toad is thrown up into the air, and lands on the plank with a sufficient force to kill it. The bones are then dried while being carried on the person. On a moonlit night at midnight, and all alone, the would-be toadman goes to a stream where he throws in the bones, which let out such screams that only a brave man can stand for it. One bone, still screaming, points or even moves upstream. This bone must be taken out of the water, and carried about by the toadman who is now in league with the Devil. According to one account the toadman must take the bone to the stables at midnight for three nights running, when on the third night he meets the devil, fights him, and draws blood. He is then, and not before, a fully-fledged toadman. He will be marked out as an aloof, silent fellow with strange supernatural powers.[72]

The folk magic that lay behind the toadbone ritual had learned antecedents in the grimoires (books of ritual magic) of necromancers. A love spell in a sixteenth-century manuscript now in the Folger Shakespeare Library contains a very similar ritual

---

70 G. W. Pattison (1953) 'Adult education and folklore', *Folklore*, 64, pp. 424–6, at p. 426.
71 Pattison (1953), p. 425.
72 Pattison (1953), p. 425.

procedure, except it is supposed to give the practitioner control over women rather than animals (albeit toadmen were supposed to have power over women as well):

> Take a frog that is using to dry land and put him in a pot, that is made full of holes and stop it fast. Then bury the pot in a cross highway in an anthill, with something, and let it be there nine days and look thou stop it fast, and that thou goest against the wind that it hear no noise, and at the nine days' end go and take out the pot, and thou shalt find two bones in it, take them and put them in a running water, and one of them will float against the stream. Mark it well but keep them both, and make thee a ring, and take part of that it swum against the stream, and set it in the ring, and when thou wilt have any woman and put it on her right hand, or else touch her therewith, and she shall never rest until she hath been with thee &c. If thou wilt no more of her, and will have her to go away, touch her with the other bone, and she will not tarry with thee.[73]

Elements of the rite can also be found in the Peterborough Lapidary, although here its purpose is to obtain the toadstone, supposedly found on the toad's head and an antidote to poison: 'take the toad and put him in a new earthenware pot, and make many holes in it, and put it in an ant hill, and cover over the pot; and then the ants will eat all of the toad except the bones, and you will find the stone stuck on the head of the toad'.[74] The toadbone ritual's derivation from learned magic means that its popular use may date from the seventeenth century, when a growth in popular literacy meant that books of magic (written in English rather than Latin) fell into the hands of cunning-men and cunning-women.[75] The ritual is likely to have evolved its agricultural rather than amorous application as a result of the particular needs of rural communities.

Counter-witchcraft and cunning-folk

Whether or not any people in the Peterborough area continued to believe they were witches after the era of the witch trials, many people certainly carried on believing that it was worth protecting themselves from the supposed witchcraft of others. Counter-witchcraft – apotropaic practices and behaviours designed to ward off evil – endured well into the twentieth century. In 1957 a man from Thorney recounted that his great aunt, who was born in 1875:

> once told him that when she was a child her mother had always made her wear a knot of scarlet ribbon pinned to her underwear. This was to protect her against witchcraft. She had, however, ceased to wear the ribbon from the time of her marriage because her husband had laughed at her for being so superstitious.[76]

73 D. Harms, J. R. Clark and J. H. Peterson (eds) (2015) *The Book of Oberon: A Sourcebook of Elizabethan Magic*, Woodbury, Minn.: Llewellyn, p. 501. There is an almost identical spell, using a mole instead of a toad, in another sixteenth-century grimoire in Cambridge University Library (see Foreman (2015), p. 60).
74 Young (2016a), p. 28. On traditions of toad magic see Andrew D. Chumbley (2012) *The Leaper Between: An Historical Study of the Toad-bone Amulet*, Three Hands Press, pp. 21, 26–9.
75 See Davies (2003).
76 Porter (1969), p. 182.

Counter-witchcraft, or 'unwitching', was the realm of cunning-folk (sometimes called, inaccurately, white witches) who provided their clients with services such as finding lost objects by magic and magical thief detection. The 'village doctress' of John Clare's poem of that title, with her extensive traditional knowledge of plants and herbal lore, may have been such a practitioner (although Clare does not mention other services associated with cunning-folk).[77]

In 1867 a Lincolnshire farmer's wife, Mrs Smith, declared her intention to visit a wisewoman in Peterborough who could reveal the faces of criminals in a looking glass, because a five pound note had gone missing from her work box. Her cook, Sarah Digby, overheard her say this and attempted to poison her in an effort to prevent her visiting Peterborough – presumably because she knew the wisewoman would see her face in the mirror.[78] Charles Dack noted that:

When a wise woman ... is called upon to attend and charm anyone, the person to be operated upon must have an earnest belief that a cure will be effected, and the words 'Please' and 'Thank you' must not be used or the charm fails. In some cases the charmer blesses or hallows cords or leather thongs which the patient wore tied round the neck.[79]

Cunning-folk also provided love charms, although Dack observed that in the early twentieth century, chemists (the successors of the apothecaries) were expected to provide the ingredients for traditional charms as well. A Peterborough chemist was asked by a woman from the countryside for a 'pennorth of Dragons Blood' that she could place wrapped in paper under her pillow, which would ensure her husband came back to her again.[80] Dragon's Blood is a special kind of tree resin from the island of Socotra in the Arabian Gulf and, although it was a staple of the old apothecaries, was less likely to be seen in a twentieth-century chemist's shop.

Most protections against witchcraft were simple and domestic in nature. Dack observed that 'Knives crossed and laid on the floor is a strong protection against the power of witchcraft':

A very old woman once told me she once tried the knives on one of her neighbours, as she suspected the woman of overlooking her: so she asked the woman to come and see her one day but before the woman came into the house she crossed two knives and put them on the floor in a dark corner. When the suspected person came in she wouldn't sit down and soon left, appearing to be very uncomfortable; so she was a 'wrong un' but the old lady said she was all right after that and had no more trouble.[81]

77 See Rodney Lines (1986) 'John Clare and herbal medicine', *John Clare Society Journal*, 5, pp. 16–21, at p. 17.
78 *Liverpool Daily Post*, Tuesday 19 November 1867, p. 7, quoted in Emma Kay (2015) *Dining with the Victorians: A Delicious History*, Stroud: Amberley, p. 36.
79 Dack (1911), p. 25.
80 Dack (1911), p. 31.
81 Dack (1911), p. 30.

Another form of counter-witchcraft was to cross straws in the path of a suspected witch; Dack recalled that 'Many years since I remember hearing of this being done as a suspected woman was coming along, and it was said the woman got very angry and foamed at the mouth but she didn't pass the straws'.[82] Carrying a mole's foot or a magnet in the pocket was also supposed to be a protection against witchcraft.[83] Indeed, it is likely that many of the practices deemed to avert 'bad luck' by the beginning of the twentieth century had once been protections against witchcraft but had lost their original meaning.

Drumming up the dead

A strange rite with echoes of necromancy was recorded by Charles Dack as having taken place as recently as the 1850s on the River Nene. The method was used to detect and reveal the bodies of suicides who had drowned themselves in the River Nene, so that the bodies could be taken for burial in a nearby churchyard:

> A loaf of bread with quicksilver [mercury] inside has even recently been put on the river when anyone has been drowned, with the idea of its floating until it is over the body, when it stops; and about forty years ago [in the 1850s], a man told me, when his uncle committed suicide and the body could not be found, that a man with a drum was put in a boat which kept close to the loaf of bread, and was drumming all the time, and the idea was that the drummer would cause the body to float. He says, his uncle's body did not come to the surface.[84]

The use of a loaf of bread in this rite is suggestive of an offering of some sort to the dead person; the belief that the soul of the suicide remains trapped in or around their body was current in most European countries, and made it easier for a necromancer to raise the soul of a suicide than any other person. The addition of drumming to the rite has echoes of the practices of shamans in Lapland and Siberia, who beat a drum to raise the spirits who then communicate through them. However, it is well-nigh impossible to establish whether the resemblance of the practice recorded by Dack to these kinds of ancient necromancy was in any way intentional.

Witchcraft in modern Peterborough

It seems unlikely that traditional belief in witchcraft survives in the Peterborough area, as it already seems to have been vanishing in the period after the Second World War, when folklorists such as G. W. Pattison were collecting stories from elderly people. Agricultural mechanisation and the introduction of technology have removed many of the unpredictable features of rural life that contributed to belief in witchcraft. However, belief in witchcraft survives in other ways. In the 2011 Census, just under

82   Dack (1911), p. 31.
83   Dack (1911), p. 33.
84   Dack (1899), p. 339.

0.1 per cent of people in Peterborough Unitary Authority described their religion as 'pagan', and paganism emerged as the seventh largest religion in England and Wales, with around 57,000 people choosing to describe their beliefs in this way.[85] However, the number of contemporary pagans is probably much greater, since many people are still reluctant to admit publicly to their beliefs.

The largest group of contemporary pagans follow the Wiccan religion, popularised in the 1950s by Gerald Gardner after the 1735 Witchcraft Act was repealed in 1951. The 1735 Act had made it illegal for anyone to claim to be a witch, although it did not treat witchcraft as a real phenomenon. Wiccan beliefs differ considerably from traditional English belief in witchcraft – most notably by claiming that witchcraft is a force for good, and portraying witches as worshippers of a goddess – but the religion grew considerably in popularity from the 1960s onwards. In 1988 the anthropologist Vinay Srivastava recounted meeting a man named Dennis living in Peterborough who considered himself a hereditary witch in the 'Elven tradition' and was looking for a suitably qualified woman to become the high priestess of a coven he intended to set up in the city.[86] In 2010 a local Wiccan spoke publicly about her religion to the *Peterborough Telegraph*,[87] but although Wiccans undoubtedly live in Peterborough, the religion is not prominent in the city.

In the second half of the twentieth century Peterborough was the recipient of a number of immigrant communities, starting with Italians from southern Italy and Sicily, where a strong belief in the 'evil eye' prevails. Whether such beliefs have survived in Peterborough's Italian community, who arrived in the 1950s to work in the brickfields, would make an interesting study. However, belief in the possibility of black magic would appear to persist in Peterborough's Pakistani Muslim community. A guide to working with people of Pakistani descent produced by Cambridgeshire and Peterborough NHS Trust notes that, within Pakistani culture, mental illness may be interpreted spiritually (perhaps as possession by a *jinni* or the result of the evil eye), and may be treated by spiritual therapists practising ancient techniques of counter-witchcraft known as *ruqyah*.[88] A quick web search reveals that demand for *ruqyah* does indeed exist in Peterborough, but any analysis of the prevalence of such beliefs in the city would require a proper anthropological study that lies beyond the scope of this book. Nevertheless, it would seem that belief in witchcraft and magic is alive and well in modern Peterborough, even if hidden beneath the surface.

85 'How religion has changed in England and Wales', Office for National Statistics, visual.ons.gov.uk/2011-census-religion, retrieved 8 December 2016.

86 Vinay K. Srivastava (1988) 'Ethnographic notebook: modern witchcraft and occultism in Cambridge', *Cambridge Journal of Anthropology*, 13, pp. 50–71, at p. 56. In Wicca a coven consists of 13 people and is led by a high priestess, representing the Goddess, and a man representing the Horned God.

87 Carly Lewthwaite, 'Dispelling the myths about the Wiccan religion', *Peterborough Telegraph*, online edn, 21 October 2010, retrieved 8 December 2016.

88 Shama Kama and Stuart Whomsley (2011) *Working with Pakistani Service Users and Their Families: A Practitioner's Guide*, Cambridgeshire and Peterborough NHS Foundation Trust, pp. 15–16.

Chapter 3
Folklore in and around Peterborough

This chapter provides a guide to folklore associated with particular places in the Peterborough region, starting with the parish of Peterborough St John (which anciently covered the whole city) and then proceeding alphabetically through the parishes (not all of which are civil parishes today).

Peterborough St John

Finger holes in the Hedda Stone

One of the few surviving relics of the monastery of Medeshamstede founded by King Peada in 654 is the so-called Hedda Stone (or Monks' Stone), currently located in the 'New Building' behind the high altar of Peterborough Minster. This stone was set up by Godric, abbot of Crowland, in the ruins of Medeshamstede after its destruction by the Danes in 869 as a memorial to the monks whose bodies he buried. Gunton recorded a curious custom of seventeenth-century tourists putting their fingers in the stone:

Figure 11 The Hedda Stone in Peterborough Minster. Photograph by the author.

The stone is still remaining … which, as it was at first, called by the name of the place, Medeshamsted; so it is now amongst some, known by the name of Peterburgh: and there being certain little holes in the sides of the stone, it was lately a merry custom for strangers, to put their fingers into one of those holes, that they might say, they had been at Peterburgh.[1]

There are indeed four small circular holes in the stone which appear to have been worn by constant touching. The fact that people said they had 'been at Peterborough' when they put their fingers in the stone may be a joke based on the fact that the Middle English word 'burgh' meant both a town and a small hill, and the shape of the Hedda Stone makes it look a little like a small hill. On the other hand, the fame of the stone combined with the holes may simply have tempted people to insert their fingers in the same way visitors to Rome traditionally put their hands in the Bocca della Verita.

Tombs of two queens

Peterborough Minster is famous for being the site of the burials of two queens: Katharine of Aragon, buried in 1536, and Mary, Queen of Scots, who was buried at Peterborough between 1587 and 1612, when her son King James I had her body moved to Westminster Abbey. The site of the tomb of Henry VIII's first wife, on the south side of the north choir ambulatory, is one of the Minster's major tourist attractions, with an annual festival in the queen's honour. However, it seems that the tomb of the tragic queen has always been a draw for visitors. In the seventeenth century not only the tomb but also the queen's hearse could still be seen. The hearse would have been the carriage, covered in black cloth, which was used to bring Katharine's body to Peterborough Minster on 29 January 1536. Gunton reported that 'her Hearse [was] covered with a black Velvet Pall, crossed with white Cloth of silver', but this was replaced at a date unknown to Gunton with 'one of meaner value … with her Spanish Scutcheons affixed thereunto'. Even this was destroyed or taken away by Oliver Cromwell's soldiers in 1643.[2]

Gunton thought – as many have since – that Peterborough Minster only survived the dissolution on account of Katharine's tomb, whose presence made Henry more willing to turn the abbey church into a cathedral.[3] Because she resisted Henry VIII's claim that he had the right to divorce her without the Pope's permission, Katharine was venerated as a saintly figure after her death by Catholics, but it would seem that her reputation for sanctity also lingered on amongst the population in general. In 1696 the father of English folklore, John Aubrey (1626–1697) reported an apparently

1   Gunton (1686), pp. 8–9.
2   Gunton (1686), p. 57.
3   On the other hand, Henry did not spare the abbey church at Bury St Edmunds where his beloved youngest sister Mary Rose Tudor was buried in 1533, and the creation of the Diocese of Peterborough was in line with earlier plans drawn up by Cardinal Wolsey for the division of the Diocese of Lincoln into smaller and more manageable territories.

Figure 12 The tomb of Katharine of Aragon in Peterborough Minster. Photograph by the author.

miraculous cure at Katharine's tomb that must have taken place before 1643 (since the hearse was taken away in that year):

> William Backhouse of Swallowfield in Berkshire Esq had an ugly Scab that grew on the middle of his Forehead, which had been there for some Years, and he could not be Cured; it became so nauseous, that he would see none but his intimate Friends: He was a Learned Gentleman, a Chimist and Antiquary: His custom was, once every Summer to Travel to see Cathedrals, Abbeys, Castles, &c. In his Journey, being come to Peterborough, he dreamt there, that he was in a Church and saw a Hearse, and that one did bid him wet his Scab, with the drops of the Marble. The next Day he went to Morning-Service, and afterwards going about the Church, saw the very Hearse (which was of Black Say, for Queen Katharine, Wife to King Henry VIII.) and the Marble Grave-Stone by. He found drops on the Marble, and there were some Cavities wherein he dip'd his Finger, and wetted the Scab: In Seven Days it was perfectly Cured. This accurate and certain Information, I had from my worthy Friend Elias Ashmole Esq who called Mr. Backhouse Father, and had this Account from his own Mouth. (May Dew is a great Dissolvent.)[4]

---

4   John Aubrey (1696) *Miscellanies*, London, pp. 100–1.

The idea that cures can be obtained in dream visions is an ancient one that dates back to the practice of 'incubation' in ancient Greece, which meant sleeping within the precincts of a shrine in the hope that the god (usually Aesculapius, the god of healing) would visit a person and heal them during the night. The practice survived into Christianity; at St Bartholomew's Hospital in Smithfield, founded in 1123, patients hoped for curative dream visions of St Bartholomew.[5] Sick pilgrims likewise made their way to the tomb of King Henry VI at Windsor with the same hope.[6] Aubrey did not report the identity of the anonymous 'one' who instructed Backhouse to wet his scab from the tomb, but according to the tradition of incubation dreams the visitant would be the queen herself.

Gunton recorded that 'shortly after' the burial of Mary, Queen of Scots a table with a Latin inscription was set up over the tomb. The text was, implicitly, extremely critical of Elizabeth I for executing her cousin and accused the queen of undermining the dignity of monarchs everywhere:

> Mary Queen of Scots, daughter of a King, Widow of the King of France, Cousin, and next heir to the Queen of England, adorned with Royal vertues, and a Royal mind (the right of Princes being oftentimes in vain implored) by barbarous, and Tyrannical cruelty, the ornament of our age and truly Royal light, is extinguished. By the same unrighteous judgment, both Mary Queen of Scots, with natural death, and all surviving Kings (now made common persons) are punished with civil death. A strange and unusual kind of monument this is, wherein the living are included with the dead: For, with the sacred ashes of this blessed Mary, know, that the Majesty of all Kings, and Princes, lieth here violated, and prostrate. And because Regal secrecy doth enough and more admonish Kings of their duty, Traveller, I say no more.[7]

Perhaps the fact that the text was in Latin meant that whoever set it up was able to get away with such open criticism of Elizabeth, but Gunton noted that the table did not remain for long, implying that it may already have disappeared when James I removed his mother's body to Westminster Abbey. The 'Royal Ensigns of an Helmet, Sword, and Scutcheon' disappeared in the ransacking of 1643. In the 1660s Matthew Pool recorded a tradition that it had been unlucky to the House of Stuart to move the queen's body:

> *Thomas Fludd,* of *Kent,* Esq; told me, That it is an old Observation, which was pressed earnestly to King *James* I. that he should not remove the Queen of *Scots* Body from

---

5   Basil Clarke (1975) *Mental Disorder in Earlier Britain: Exploratory Studies,* Cardiff: University of Wales Press, pp. 144–7.

6   Clarke (1975), pp. 163–5.

7   Translation in Gunton (1686), p. 80. The original text read *Maria Scotorum Regina, Regis filia, Regis Gallorum. / Vidua, Reginae Angliae Agnata, & Haeres proxima: / Virtutibus Regiis, & animo Regio ornata, jure Regio / Frustra saepius implorato, barbara, & tyrannica / Crudelitate ornamentum nostri seculi, & lumen / Vere Regium extinguitur: Eodem nefario judicio / Et Maria Scotorum Regina morte naturali, & omnes / Superstites Reges, plebeii facti, morte civili mulctantur. / Novum, & inauditum tumuli genus, in quo, cum vivis / Mortui includuntur, hic extat: Cum sacris enim Divae / Mariae cineribus, omnium Regum, at[que] Principum vio- / latam, at[que] prostratam Majestatem hic jacere scito: / Et quia tacitum Regale satis super[que] Reges sui / Officii monet, plura non addo, Viator.*

Figure 13 Site of the former tomb of Mary, Queen of Scots in Peterborough Minster. Photograph by the author.

Northampton-shire, where she was Beheaded, and Interred. For that it always bodes ill to the Family, when Bodies are remov'd from their Graves. For some of the Family will die shortly after, as did Prince *Henry,* and, I think, Queen *Anne.*[8]

The exhumation of the queen's body took place on 11 October 1612, and James's eldest son Henry, Prince of Wales, died of typhoid on 6 November. Queen Anne of Denmark, however, did not die until 1619. There seems to have been another contradictory local story about Mary's tomb in circulation when Daniel Defoe visited the city in the 1720s. Defoe noted that 'some do not stick to tell us, that tho' the Monument [in Westminster Abbey] was erected, the Body was never removed'.[9]

Old Scarlett

One of the best known characters of Peterborough Minster was the sexton, Robert Scarlett (1496–1594), known as 'Old Scarlett', whose portrait, accompanied by verses in his memory, appears above the Minster's west door. Scarlett's principal claim to fame, besides his unusual longevity, was that he buried two queens – Katharine of Aragon in 1536 and Mary, Queen of Scots in 1587. The seventeenth-century historian Thomas

---

8   William Turner (1697) *A Compleat History of the Most Remarkable Providences both of Judgment and Mercy, Which Have Hapned in this Present Age,* London, p. 77.

9   Daniel Defoe (1748) *A Tour thro' the Whole Island of Great Britain,* 4 vols, London, p. 30.

Fuller noted that some ascribed Scarlett's longevity to his exposure to decaying corpses: 'though sextons often met with bad savours, arising from corpses, too much (or rather too little) corrupted, yet in the instance of his long life, alleged by such who maintain that the smelling to perfect mould, made of men's consumed bodies, is a preservation of life'.[10] The present portrait of Scarlett hanging above the south-western door was made in 1665 to replace the commemorative mural above the north-western door, dating from around 1600, which was defaced by Parliamentarian soldiers in 1643.[11]

The Paschal Pickerel

The 'paschal pickerel' seems to have been a standing joke in Peterborough before the destruction of the medieval stained glass windows of the Minster by Cromwell's soldiers in 1643. Although images in churches were outlawed in the reign of King Edward VI (1547–53), stained glass windows often survived because it was so expensive to reglaze a church, especially a huge one like Peterborough Minster. This meant that post-Reformation people were able to admire and appreciate surviving medieval windows, some of which became famous, although not always for the reasons one might expect. Simon Patrick, the editor of Gunton's *History of the Church of Peterburgh*, told the story of the paschal pickerel:

> And amongst other things thus demolisht in the Windows, there was one thing Fame had made very remarkable, and that was the story of the Paschal Pickeril. The thing was this; Our Saviour was represented in two places, in the Cloyster and in the great Western Window, sitting at his last Supper with his twelve Apostles; In one place there was a single Fish, in the other three Fishes in a Dish, set before him. This occasion'd that discourse and common Talk, I remember, I have often heard, of the Paschal Pickeril at Peterburgh. Now what should be the meaning of this conceit, is left to every one to conjecture. The Account that I have had from some was this, That it was the device of some devout and ignorant Artist, from a Notion he had of the time this last Supper must needs be in, that is of Lent, and that our Saviour himself was a strict observer of Lent, and eat no Flesh all that season: and therefore He took liberty, to substitute a Fish instead of the Paschal Lamb. Whatever it was, the matter of Fact was certain: and that particular piece of Glass wherein the Three Fishes are portray'd happend to be preserved in the great Devastation, and was committed to my trust by the Author of the foregoing History [Gunton], from whom I had this Relation, and is yet to be seen.[12]

Maundy Thursday, when the Last Supper was commemorated by the medieval church, was not in fact considered one of the fast days of Lent, which makes the appearance of fish in the depiction of the Last Supper even stranger. Perhaps the artist was unable to resist a reference to fishing, which was one of Peterborough's main sources of income before the drainage of the Fens.

---

10   George Dixon (1980) *Old Scarlett*, Peterborough: Annakin, p. 21.
11   Dixon (1980), p. 17.
12   Gunton (1686), p. 337. It is not known what happened to the surviving piece of stained glass preserved by Dean Patrick.

St Leonard's Well

In addition to St Laurence's Well near the monastic infirmary, where pilgrimages seem to have been suppressed in the thirteenth century and which was subsequently forgotten, Peterborough had another holy well which survived the Reformation. A leper hospital was established just outside the city in the twelfth century dedicated to St Leonard, but the nearby St Leonard's Well seems to have retained its reputation even after the dissolution of the hospital along with the rest of Peterborough's monastic institutions in 1539. The hospital building was still standing in Gunton's day, and he reported that 'There is still a Well near the Spittle [i.e. hospital], which is called St. Leonard's Well, whose water hath been thought Medicinal'.[13] This suggests that the well was still a place of pilgrimage in the seventeenth century. Unfortunately, St Leonard's Hospital has been obliterated so completely that even the street named after the vanished hospital, St Leonard's Street, was destroyed by the construction of Bourges Boulevard in the early 1980s. The site of the hospital and well lies somewhere between the Crescent Bridge and Westgate roundabouts.

Divine retribution

Gunton recorded a popular story that the Parliamentarian soldiers who desecrated and defaced the Minster in 1643 suffered divine retribution for firing their muskets at the ceiling, although he was unable to confirm it as true:

> In the Roof of the Church, in a large Oval yet to be seen, was the Picture of our Saviour seated on a Throne, one hand erected, and holding a Globe in the other: attended with the four Evangelists and Saints on each side, with Crowns in their hands .... Some of the company espying this, cry out and say, Lo this is the God these People bow and cringe unto; This is the Idol they worship and adore. Hereupon several Souldiers charge their Muskets, (amongst whom one Daniel Wood of Captain Ropers Company was the chief) and discharge them at it: and by the many shots they made, at length do quite deface and spoil [the] Picture. The odiousness of this Act gave occasion (I suppose) to a common Fame very rife at that time, ... viz. That divine Vengeance had signally seised on some of the principal Actors, That one was struck blind upon the place by a Re-bound of his Bullet; That another dyed mad a little after; neither of which I can certainly attest. For, though I have made it my business to enquire of this, I could never find any other judgment befal them then, but that of a mad blind Zeal, wherewith these persons were certainly possest.[14]

The bells of St John's

According to an old rhyme, collected by Charles Dack from an old lady, it was bad luck for the bells of the Minster and the bells of St John's church to strike together:

> When the clock of the Abbey strikes three minutes fast,
> There will be a gay wedding before the month's past;

---

13   Gunton (1686), p. 317.
14   Gunton (1686), pp. 334–5.

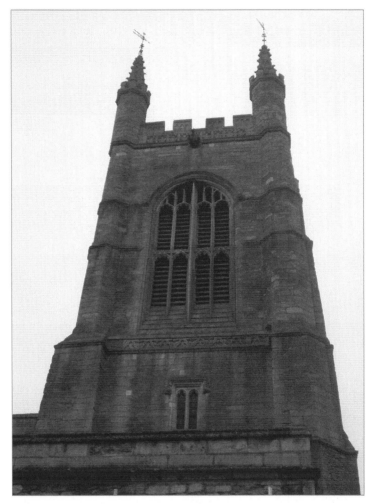

Figure 14 The belfry of St John's church, Peterborough. Photograph by the author.

When the clock of the Abbey strikes three minutes slow,
The river's bright waters will soon overflow;
When the Church Clock and Abbey Clock strike both together,
There will soon be a death or a change in the weather.

In the late nineteenth century the head verger of the Cathedral always ensured that the clock of St John's was kept slightly faster than that of the Minster. When the vicar of St John's asked him why this was, the verger replied, 'Well Vicar, you know, the other disciple did outrun St. Peter on the way to the tomb, so St. John has always kept in front ever since.'[15] This was a joke based on the Minster's dedication to St Peter and the parish church's dedication to St John – although since the parish church is actually dedicated to St John the Baptist, the verger's jest was imperfect. St John's once had

---

15   Dack (1911), p. 6.

a 'gleaning bell' which was rung at 5.45am and 8.45pm, but according to Dack the ringing of this bell was discontinued 'about thirty or forty years since' (in the 1860s or 1870s).[16]

Revenants, ghosts, burials and bodysnatchers

The Minster precincts retained an old-fashioned night-watchman until well into the nineteenth century. Dack suggested that he became something of a figure of fun:

> The last night-watchman of the old school passed away about fifteen years since [c. 1884], and until he was totally incapable, he occupied his box in the Minster precincts, and went round regularly, calling out the hours and state of the weather: unless he was fast asleep, or some young men had played a trick upon him of fastening him in his box, or even pushing it over and sitting on it, so that the poor man could not get out.[17]

In 1904 a local newspaper recalled a story whose protagonist was presumably the same old Minster night-watchman:

> A watchman was making his beat of the Minster Yard one night, sonorously proclaiming the state of the weather for any sleepless citizen who might hear him, when he was rooted to the ground with fear. Not far from the gaol the ground suddenly began to crack and heave. Visions of spirits of dead abbots and priors, and monks rose before the watchman's terror-stricken mind as the heaving ground opened and a body rose from its grave and disappeared in the darkness. Next morning the watchman was found where he had fallen, but that he had been the victim of no mere fancy was clear, for there was the gruesome hole in the earth from which the body had risen. An examination, however, of the adjacent gaol revealed the fact that the only prisoner, a man, had disappeared – he had burrowed his way out![18]

False revenants in the form of escaping prisoners were not the city's only problem with the unquiet dead. 'Resurrectionists' or bodysnatchers, who exhumed and sold freshly buried corpses to surgeons and anatomy students, were much feared in the early nineteenth century. In 1905 a very elderly resident of the city recollected that there was a particular problem at Cowgate cemetery, which was opened in 1803 to relieve pressure on burials in the Minster Yard:

> When my mother, Margaret Bothway White, died on December 10th, 1831, two men were employed for twelve days to watch her grave in the old graveyard in Cowgate. One was armed with a pistol and dagger, and the other kept him company during the night. The Cowgate Graveyard was then walled round, which made it easier to disinter

---

16 Dack (1899), p. 339.
17 Dack (1899), p. 541.
18 'How our grandfathers did it', *Peterborough Advertiser*, 5 March 1904, newspaper cutting in CUL, Lib.5.89.520–1, p. 65.

the bodies and send them away for anatomical purpose. There was a nice little set in Newton who used to make money out of it.[19]

Peterborough was also the scene of unconventional burials. In 1811 a twenty-two year old woman, Elizabeth James, took arsenic after a failed romance and was buried by six female relatives at the crossroads of Crawthorne Lane (now Burghley Road) and Park Road. The spot became known as 'the Girl's Grave' and was marked by a small stone in a garden, although this was no longer visible by the end of the nineteenth century. According to the newspapers that reported the event, the female mourners wore white (traditional at the funeral of a young woman who died a virgin),[20] and the burial of Elizabeth James is a peculiar example of an attempt to show reverence (the white mourning clothes and the gravestone) while at the same time observing the old custom of burying a suicide in unconsecrated ground at the crossroads (traditionally believed to deter the spirit haunting the living, as it would be unable to find its way).

In January 1892 an alarming series of hauntings at a small terraced house, 22 Mayor's Walk, on the west side of the city, was reported in the *Peterborough Advertiser*. Built for and primarily occupied by employees of the Great Eastern Railway, number 22 was occupied by the Rimes family and their lodgers. Towards the end of 1891 the family began experiencing the typical phenomena associated with 'poltergeist' hauntings, in the form of loud and unexplained knockings and mysterious footsteps. Just after Christmas, Mr and Mrs Rimes encountered another railway employee named Arthur Wilson, who offered to spend the night in the house on 29 December 1891. Hearing a noise from the passage in the night, Wilson left his room and found the passage silent; then he heard a noise behind him like a 'huge sack of coals toppled pell-mell down the stairs'. The neighbours described it as sounding like a cannon being fired, and feared number 22 might collapse. Wilson never returned and the Rimes family moved out of the house soon afterwards.[21]

Hare coursing in the Minster Yard

Some time in the 1840s or 1850s Jack Raveley, a local Peterborough character renowned for his speed, personally pursued and caught a hare in the Minster precincts, partly because the presence of a hare in the precincts was considered unlucky:

> In those days hares would frequently make their way from the fields to feed on the rich pasturage in the Minster Close. Experience has shown that in spite of the vast increase in population hares are still found foolish enough to run the same risk. It is probable, however, that these visitants from the local game preserves in the neighbourhood were not frequent, for a local adage that

---

19 'Telephone talks – or, local notabilities rung up', *Saturday Citizen*, 2 December 1905, newspaper cutting in CUL, Lib.5.89.520–1, pp. 210.

20 Robert Halliday (2010) 'The roadside burial of suicides: an East Anglian study', *Folklore*, 121, pp. 81–93, at p. 85.

21 For a full account of the Mayor's Walk poltergeist see Orme (2012), pp. 60–2.

Figure 15 The Minster Yard, site of all Peterborough burials until 1803. Photograph by the author.

> If in the Minster Close a hare
> Should for itself have made a lair,
> Be sure before the week is down
> A fire will rage within the town.

But one day it was reported that a hare was in the Minster Close. Before the local sportsmen had time to turn out with their guns, Raveley had heard the news, and had conceived the idea of enjoying a coursing match to himself. Accordingly he repaired to the Minster Yard, and presently the hare made its appearance. Raveley was quickly in pursuit. Away went the hare, over the tombstones and through the bushes, first into one corner and then into another. Raveley was after it, keeping close up to it; no greyhound could have followed better. Hour after hour went by, but still the chase continued; the hare was evidently getting puffed, but Raveley was fresh and still eager in the chase. The result was that after several hours coursing the hare had to succumb; Raveley pounced upon it and seized his prize in triumph, and received the applause of numbers of people who had witnessed this strange coursing match.[22]

Election days

Elections in the eighteenth and early nineteenth centuries were very boisterous and raucous affairs, with the candidates openly bribing the electors with food and drink. A cartoon preserved in the British Museum satirises Matthew Wyldbore, MP for Peterborough between 1768 and 1780, portraying him as a wild boar ridden by a woman holding a lap dog while a man with stag's horns leads the boar by a ring in its nose. Money bags hanging from the man's horns read '£500 1768' and '£1000 1774', a reference to the fact that Wyldbore had to bribe his electors twice as much to get re-elected in 1774 as he had in 1768, and was consequently being 'led by the nose' by them.[23]

In 1905 an elderly resident recollected that supporters of Sir Robert Heron (1765–1854), who was MP for Peterborough between 1819 and 1847:

> [G]ot a heron from Milton Park, stuffed it, and carried it at the head of all processions. The other party had the effigy of a Bishop in his robes and all, of course, carried flags … When the processions met there were some rare scenes. The Bishop's effigy came off badly, and the heron was triumphant. There were bands of music, and bandsmen all joined in the fray, and ended by having all the drum heads knocked in'.[24]

Sir Robert was a Whig, and his opponents carried an effigy of a bishop because the senior clergy (including the bishops of Peterborough) tended to support the Tories.

Another Peterborough custom on election day was the destruction of the polling booths in the marketplace after polls closed at 4pm. Before the Great Reform Act of 1832, voting in Peterborough was restricted to a tiny minority, and even after 1832 wealth qualifications were required to vote. Anger at this injustice may have lain behind the symbolic violence done to the booths on polling day. The Ballot Act of 1872, which introduced secret ballots, finally did away with the custom. Dack described vividly what used to happen:

> The hustings and polling-booths were erected in front of the Guildhall, and as 4 o'clock approached the market-place got more and more crowded, and the nearer the time the more dense was the mass of people next the booth, the rougher element being particularly conspicuous. As the hands of the clock neared the hour, there was a silence which was oppressive. Those in the booth had been carefully getting out, until no one was left inside but the necessary clerks and officers and last voters. But at the sound of

---

22 Saunders (1888), pp. 232–3.
23 British Museum collections online, britishmuseum.org/research/collection_online/collection_object_ details.aspx?objectId=1452765&partId=1, retrieved 22 December 2016.
24 'Telephone talks – or, local notabilities rung up', *Saturday Citizen*, 2 December 1905, newspaper cutting in CUL, Lib.5.89.520–1, pp. 209.

the first stroke of four, a sudden rasping, crashing, wrenching noise of tearing wood was heard; each one left in the hustings was getting out anyhow, jumping or rushing as fast as possible; books, papers, and other things were thrown to other responsible people in the building, for it was *sauve qui peut*; within two minutes not a vestige of the hustings remained, but men, women, and boys might be seen carrying away pieces of deal or other wood in all directions, and the old Town Hall was soon left without a hideous wooden structure to hide its quaintness. No tools were allowed: only hands, and the wood from the structure. It was a sight intensely amusing, exciting, and much appreciated. The windows round the square were filled with spectators, eagerly looking on and encouraging those in whom they took an interest, to go in and win. Very few fights took place, as the gainer of the wood was generally satisfied with one piece; but, if greedy and wanting more, some would carefully hide the first piece and rush back for a second – during their absence some keen observer had taken the first piece from its hiding-place, and left the original owner to find himself without anything.[25]

UFOs over Peterborough

'Unidentified flying objects' or UFOs are a staple of contemporary folklore throughout the western world, although in spite of the acronym's literal meaning it has become a synonym for suspected extraterrestrial activity. Long before UFOs were associated with aliens, however, reports of them channelled fears of new and terrible weapons being developed by foreign powers in the run-up to the First World War. One of the earliest reports of a mysterious object in the sky came from Peterborough, where at 5.15am on 23 March 1909 police constable Kettle 'saw a powerful light and heard the sound of a high-powered engine'. Kettle described the object as 'travelling at a rapid speed, at a height of 1,200 feet. The light was carried by a narrow oblong-shaped dark-coloured craft.' Two nights later an engine driver at March spotted 'an airship with powerful lights attached to it' coming from the direction of Peterborough, 'moving at a good pace even though it looked to be fighting a heavy wind'.

The police dismissed the sightings as a kite with a Chinese lantern attached to it, explaining away the sound of the motor as one from a bakery in Cobden Street. However, further sightings prompted a reporter from the *Daily Express* to tour the roads around Peterborough 'in search of the craft and its base'.[26] Then, as now, reports of UFOs seem to have generated suspicion of a government conspiracy to develop secret weapons. It is worth noting that the Peterborough sighting followed the publication of H. G. Wells's novel *The War in the Air*, about a future aerial conflict between Britain and Germany, in serial form in *Pall Mall* magazine in 1908. Then, as now, popular culture stimulated interest in and reports of UFOs. Peterborough has been the sight of many reported UFO sightings since, but none as historically significant as the 'phantom airship scare' of 1909.

---

25 Dack (1899), pp. 340–1.
26 Nigel Watson (2015) *UFOs of the First World War: Phantom Airships, Balloons, Aircraft and Other Mysterious Aerial Phenomena,* Stroud: History Press, p. 18. On the Peterborough dirigible sightings see also Alfred Gollin (1989) *The Impact of Air Power on the British People and Their Government, 1909–1914,* Stanford, Calif.: Stanford University Press, p. 53.

Figure 16 Torpel Manor Field, between Ashton and Helpston. Photograph by the author.

Ashton

An apparition in Torpel Manor Field

As a young man John Clare found work at Basset's Farm in Ashton. One night, walking through Torpel Manor Field, he had a terrifying encounter with what he thought was a supernatural apparition:

> The worst fright I ever met with was on a harvest night when I workd at Bassets of Ashton[.] we was always late ere we gave over work as harvesters generally are and ere we finished our suppers it was night midnight by the time I started home which was but the distance of a short mile but I had a terror haunting spot to cross calld Baron parks in which was several ruins of roman camps and saxon castles and of course was people[d] with many mysterys of spirits[.] the tales were numberless of ghosts and goblings that were seen there and I never passd it without my memory keeping a strict eye to look for them and one night rather late I fanc[y]ed I saw somthing stand wavering in the path way but my hopes put it off as a shadow till on coming nearer I found that it was somthing but wether of flesh and blood was a question[.] my astonished terrors magnified it into a horrible figure[;] it appeard to have ears of a vas[t] length and the hair seemd to hang about it .... I trembld and almost wishd the earth woud open to hide me[.] I woud have spoke but I coud not and on attempting to pass it I gave it the road and ran off as fast as I coud and on stopping at the stile to look were it was my increasd terror found it close at my heels[.] I thought it was nothing but infernal now and scarce [know]ing what I did I took to my heels and when I got home I felt nearly fit to dye[.] I felt assurd that ghosts did exist and I dare not pass the close the

next day till quite late in the day when every body was abroad[,] when to my surprise I found it was nothing but a poor cade foal that had lost its mother.[27]

It seems likely that Clare mistook the foal for the Northamptonshire 'bogey beast' known as the Shagg'd Foal or Shagfoal (see page 79), a variant of the widespread shape-shifting water spirit (best known by its Scottish name of kelpie) that often takes the form of a horse or pony which lures travellers into danger or tempts them into mounting its back. Torpel Manor Field, here called 'Baron parks' by Clare, is now under the care of the Langdyke Countryside Trust. The 'several ruins of roman camps and saxon castles' are in fact medieval earthworks, the last remains of thirteenth-century Torpel House and its surrounding village.[28]

A will o'the wisp

One of several encounters with marsh lights or will o'the wisps recorded by John Clare (who was convinced they were spirits) took place on his way back from Ashton, and is a reminder of how alarming the chemical glow of a jack o'lantern must have appeared in a world without any artificial light other than candles:

> [O]ne night when returning home from Ashton on a courting excursion I saw one as if meeting me[;] I felt very terrified and on getting to a stile I determi[n]d to wait and see if it was a person with a lanthorn or a will o whisp[.] it came on steadily as if on the path way and when it got near me within a poles reach perhaps as I thought it made a sudden leap as if to listen to me[.] I then believed it was some one but it blazd out like a whisp of straw and made a crackling noise like straw burning which soon convinced me of its visit[.] the luminous haloo that spread from it was of a mysterious terrific hue and the enlargd size and whiteness of my own hands frit me[.] the rushes appeard to have grown up as large and tall as walebone whips and the bushes seemd to be climbing the sky[;] every thing was extorted out of its own figure and magnify[i]ed[.] the darkness all round seemd to form a circalar black wall and I fancied that if I took a step forward I shoud fall into a bottomless gulph which seemd garing all round me[,] so I held fast by the stile post till it darted away when I took to my heels and got home as fast as [I] coud.[29]

Barnack

Button Cap

'Button Cap' was a ghost reputed to haunt Barnack rectory. The Victorian novelist Charles Kingsley (1819–1875), who was brought up in the house, reported that:

> [H]e lived in the great north room at Barnack. I knew him well. He used to walk across the room in flopping slippers, and turn over the leaves of books to find the missing

---

27 Clare (2002), pp. 45–6.
28 See langdyke.org.uk/torpel-manor-field, accessed 17 December 2016.
29 Clare (2002), p. 252.

deed, whereof he had defrauded the orphan and the widow. He was an old Rector of Barnack. Everybody heard him who chose. Nobody ever saw him; but in spite of that, he wore a flowered dressing-gown, and a cap with a button on it …. Sometimes he turned cross and played Poltergeist, as the Germans say, rolling the barrels in the cellar about with surprising noise, which was undignified. So he was always ashamed of himself, and put them all back in their places before morning.[30]

J. M. Goodwin reported that the legend of Button Cap was still alive and well during the Second World War, when soldiers were billeted in the Rectory from November 1941. After the war it was discovered that the soldiers had left Button Cap a message, writing on the wall of one room: 'You old fool, you're wasting your time we have found the papers.'[31]

Shag Foal

In 1902 the natural historian George Morton was told by a woman whose family had lived at Barnack for generations that a 'Shag Foal' haunted the region, and that 'In days gone by this entity took the form of a large, black, scruffy looking bear-like animal.' The Barnack Shag Foal would lead people into dangerous marshland or lure them into mounting it, at which point it would vanish and leave the traveller 'somewhere dank, wet and inhospitable'.[32] Clare called the beast 'Old Ball' or 'the shag'd foal' and noted that 'its a common tradition in villages that the devil often appears in the form of a shag'd foal & a man in our parish [Helpston] firmly believes that he saw him in that character one morning early in harvest'.[33] Northamptonshire's Shag Foal is a variant of the better known East Anglian 'bogey beast' called variously 'Old Shuck', 'Old Shock' or 'Shucky Dog', who usually appears as a black dog but can also manifest as a spectral calf or donkey. Westwood and Simpson note that, although the name 'Shuck' derives from Old English scucca, meaning 'devil', 'shucky' also means 'shaggy' in Norfolk dialect and Shuck is frequently described as having a shaggy coat.[34]

Bottlebridge (see also Orton Longueville)

St Botolph

The manor of Bottlebridge has now been absorbed into the parish of Orton Longueville but was once a separate settlement with its own church. The name is a corruption of 'Botolph Bridge', and the Botolph Arms public house on Oundle Road is now the only reminder of the connection. The Huntingdonshire folklorist W. H. Bernard Saunders was adamant that Bottlebridge was so called because it had been the home of St Botolph (d. 655), a great East Anglian monastic saint, in the seventh century.[35] The

30   Quoted in Westwood and Simpson (2005), p. 359.
31   Clare (1996–2003), vol. 5, p. 553n.
32   Codd (2009), p. 90.
33   Quoted in Deacon (1983), p. 290.
34   Westwood and Simpson (2005), pp. 500–1.
35   Saunders (1888), p. 181.

site of Botolph's remote island monastery, Icanhoe, has never been satisfactorily identified, but no modern historian would seriously suggest Bottlebridge, since St Botolph was associated with sites much further to the east. Saunders also reported a legend that Orton Longueville parish church is partly made from the remains of Bottlebridge church:

> The late Rector of Overton Longueville (Rev. J. Watson) informed the writer that the stones which constitute the pavement in the south aisle of that Church are the gravestones taken from the old Church-yard of Bottle Bridge, and placed with the inscriptions downwards, and that the whole of the south aisle of the Church was built by materials which were brought from the ruins of Bottle Bridge.[36]

Figure 17 Sign of the Botolph Arms public house, the only surviving reminder of the old settlement of Bottlebridge. Photograph by the author.

Borough Fen

St Vincent's Cross

Between the parishes of Borough Fen, which was anciently in the Soke of Peterborough, and Thorney, which was anciently in Cambridgeshire (both are now in the Unitary Authority) stands an ancient cross that once marked the place where the three counties of Cambridgeshire, Northamptonshire and Lincolnshire met. St Vincent's or Fyrset Cross was erected after 1390 by the abbey of Crowland in Lincolnshire, after a commission was convened to examine the extent of the abbey's landholdings, and it bears four coats of arms including that of Crowland Abbey.[37] The cross was moved to its present position on the parish boundary between Thorney and Borough Fen in 1990, but a small inscribed stone still marks its original location.

---

36   Saunders (1888), p. 182.
37   David Hall (1987) *The Fenland Project, Number 2: Fenland Landscapes and Settlement between Peterborough and March*, Cambridge: Cambridgeshire Archaeological Committee, p. 54.

Figure 18 St Vincent's Cross in its original position in 1987. Photograph by and reproduced with the kind permission of David Hall.

Figure 19 (below) St Vincent's Cross today. Photograph by the author.

Boundary crosses, especially remote ones and those that marked the convergence of multiple counties, were often a focus of popular belief in buried treasure – so much so that, in 1542, a parliament of Henry VIII passed a law against people using magic to find treasure and pulling down crosses:

> If any person or persons ... use, devise, practise or exercise, or cause to be used, devised, practised or exercised, any invocations or conjurations of spirits, witchcrafts, enchantments, or sorceries, to the intent to get or find money or treasure ... or for despite of Christ, or for lucre of money, dig up or pull down any cross or crosses .... That then all and every such offence and offences ... shall be deemed accepted and adjudged felony.[38]

The government's concern stemmed partly from a worry that treasure hunters were removing important landmarks for travellers, as well as the fact that they were preventing landowners and officials of local government marking the limits of their landholdings or jurisdiction.

---

38   Quoted in Barbara Rosen (ed.) (1991) *Witchcraft in England, 1558–1618,* Amherst, Mass.: University of Massachusetts Press, pp. 53–4.

Castor and Ailsworth

St Kyneburgha of Castor

Kyneburgha was a daughter of the pagan King Penda of Mercia, who became a Christian and founded a monastery in around 650 in the ruins of the so-called 'Prae-torium', an immense C-shaped Roman building whose remains are still visible close to Castor church. The Roman road called Ermine Street ran past the Praetorium and over the fields where it crossed the Nene to the Roman town of Durobrivae, just west of the village of Water Newton on the Huntingdonshire side of the river. In the Roman period the whole area of Water Newton and Castor was a built-up industrial site where the distinctive 'Nene Valley ware' pottery was produced, but by the seventh century the area had once more become rural. According to a local legend the discoverer of Durobrivae, the pioneering archaeologist Edmund Tyrell Artis (1789–1847), was buried standing up in Castor churchyard so he could look over to the site of his most important discovery.

The course of Ermine Street is still just discernible as a raised hump across a field south of Castor church, but in previous centuries it must have been much more visible, and produced a curious legend. One of the Romanesque capitals of Castor church shows St Kyneburgha dropping a basket as she is pursued by enemies. The image seems to have generated a local folktale recorded by John Morton in 1712, who reported that Ermine Street was called by the locals 'my Lady Cony-burrow's Way', and that it ran from the river 'to the ancient Four-square well in that Churchyard at Castor'. The road was 'only a narrow Tract ... of Ground three or four Foot broad, distinguishable from the rest of the Field, thro' which it passes, by its being barrener than the Ground, on both sides of it'. According to 'an old Story that is told at Castor':

> Kinneburga's honour being attempted she fled from the Ruffian thro' those Fields: and ... the Path she took was thus miraculously mark'd out, as a Trophy of her Purity and Innocence, to be seen in future ages, and to be

Figure 20 Statue of St Kyneburgha on the exterior of Castor church. Photograph by the author.

distinguished by the name of Kinneburga's Way.[39]

Alfred Story thought that another local field name, Conegree Close, was also a corruption of Kyneburgha's name.[40] In 1737 the antiquary William Stukeley visited Castor and found that the legend of St Kyneburgha had been further transformed:

> They have still a memorial at Castor of S. Kyniburga, whom the vulgar call Lady Ketilborough, and of her coming in a coach and six, and riding over the field along the Roman road, some few nights before Michaelmas.

Stukeley noted that 15 September had been the feast of St Kyneburgha before the monks of Peterborough removed her relics to Peterborough in the eleventh century,[41] when her feast day was transferred to 7 March to celebrate her translation and those of her sisters St Kyneswitha and St Tibba.

Figure 21 (top) The grave of Edmund Tyrell Artis in Castor churchyard, supposedly buried standing up. Photograph by the author.

Figure 22 (left) St Kyneburgha dropping her basket on a Romanesque capital in Castor church. Photograph by the author.

---

39 Quoted in Westwood and Simpson (2005), pp. 360–1.
40 Story (1883), p. 35.
41 Quoted in Westwood and Simpson (2005), p. 361.

Figure 23 Ermine Street ('Lady Conyburrow's Way') running across the fields between Castor and Water Newton. Photograph by the author.

It is unclear from Stukeley's account whether the 'memorial' was an object or a custom, since 'memorial' could then mean 'commemoration' as well as its modern meaning. Either way, it is remarkable that the memory of St Kyneburgha survived the Reformation, when the cult of saints was officially stamped out. The unique dedication of Castor church, as well as Castor's lingering resentment that Peterborough had stolen its saint, may have combined with the peculiarities of the Roman landscape to preserve her memory.[42]

Robin Hood and Little John

Robin Hood and Little John are two small standing stones located in the field below the old A47 overlooking Milton Ferry Bridge (formerly known as Gunwade Ferry). The stones are low and rectangular in form, and according to Gunton were associated in local folklore with Robin Hood:

> [T]here are two long stones yet standing upon a balk in Castor-field near unto Gunwade-Ferry; which erroneous tradition hath given out to be two draughts of Arrows from Alwalton Church-yard thither; the one of Robin Hood, and the other of Little John; but

---

42 For a detailed account of legends associated with Kyneburgha, Kyneswitha and Tibba see Story (1883), pp. 28–36.

Figure 24 'Robin Hood' (foreground) and 'Little John' (background). Photograph by the author.

the truth is, they were set up for witnesses, that the carriages of Stone from Bernack to Gunwade-Ferry, to be conveyed to S. Edmunds-Bury, might pass that way without paying Toll: And in some old Terrars they are called S. Edmunds Stones. These Stones are nicked in their tops after the manner of Arrows, probably enough in memory of S. Edmund who was shot to death with arrows by the Danes.[43]

The arrows on the tops of the stones are no longer visible, but Gunton's history was quite correct. A charter of Alexander of Holderness, abbot of Peterborough 1222–26, ratifies William, son of Reginald's grant of a rod of land at 'Castorfields' to the abbot of Bury St Edmunds, and grants the abbot of St Edmunds free carriage of marble and other stone from Barnack to the River Nene between Alwalton and Peterborough in exchange for an annual payment of six shillings, instead of the usual fee demanded by the abbot of Peterborough. Since 'Robin Hood' and 'Little John' are themselves pieces of Barnack stone (known as 'rag'), it seems highly likely that the stones were intended to mark out the rod of land belonging to the abbey of Bury St Edmunds that effectively constituted the approach to a wharf from which stone was loaded onto barges to be taken into Suffolk.[44] It seems equally likely that the association between the stones and Robin Hood arose after the Reformation, when the connection with Bury St Edmunds had been forgotten but the arrows carved on the stones (the emblem of St Edmund and his abbey) suggested to local people the most famous archer of English folklore.

---

43   Gunton (1686), p. 4.
44   See Antonia Gransden (2005) *A History of the Abbey of Bury St Edmunds 1182–1256*. Woodbridge: Boydell, pp. 231–2. See also Westwood and Simpson (2005), pp. 357–9.

Burial of suicides

In 1883 John Hales recalled a peculiar tradition at Castor of burying suicides in a corner of the church. It was not unusual for a particular part of a churchyard to be set aside for suicides (or for suicides not to be buried in the churchyard at all), but it was unusual for them to be buried in the church:

> The place now occupied by the organ was used as a place for a very large plough, also for a bier for carrying the dead and generally for a rubbish heap or place for decaying flags and hassocks; also to work and letter gravestones in. The bodies of strange persons drowned such as Watermen etc, were also deposited here; I have known three persons to be so deposited. I have also seen and heard an inquest held over one of them in the church; it was over a person found drowned in a fish pond opposite the Keeper's house at the Ferry; this was in April 1840 and the coroner stood in the old writing desk.[45]

Dogsthorpe

Dogsthorpe Feast

Dogsthorpe (known interchangeably until the twentieth century as Dodsthorpe), now a built-up area of Peterborough, was for centuries a hamlet in the parish of Peterborough St John, and did not acquire its own parish church until 1957. The major event of the year in Dogsthorpe seems to have been an annual 'club feast' on the first Monday in May. Dack mentions 'village feasts' which were held in spring and early summer, beginning on a Sunday and lasting for several days, noting that 'Peterborough young people walk over to them'.[46] The *Lincolnshire Chronicle* reported in 1849 that 'A small band of music from Crowland was an acquisition, and the villagers displayed their wonted hospitality towards their friends who on that day make a point of paying them an annual visit from Peterborough and places adjacent.'[47] However, in 1844 there was a breakdown of law and order at the feast, which:

> vexatiously passed off in a manner quite different to former years, the usual quiet of the village being disturbed by several battles, fought by some of the blackguards of this city, and the parties upon whom they practised their insults. The constable was driven from the contest on the onset, and one person, apprehended by him, released from his custody.[48]

The incident may be an indication that the tradition of an open invitation to everyone from Peterborough to Dogsthorpe Feast was becoming unsustainable as the city grew in size; alternatively, a group from Peterborough may simply have used the feast as a place to settle scores. Rowdiness at traditional festivities was frequently reported in the press in the nineteenth century, and often used as an excuse for the suppression of old customs. Whether nineteenth-century revellers really were less well behaved than their

---

45   CAMUS (2004), p. 349.
46   Dack (1899), p. 338.
47   *Lincolnshire Chronicle*, 11 May 1849.
48   *Cambridge Independent Press*, 11 May 1844.

Figure 25 Woodcroft Castle. Photo by Andrew Kerr, from www.britishlistedbuildings.co.uk, via Wikimedia Commons.

predecessors is less clear; it may be that Victorian authorities were just more sensitive to public disorder than their predecessors.

Etton

Woodcroft Castle

Woodcroft Castle, in the parish of Etton, is a large thirteenth-century heavily fortified manor house surrounded by a moat. The castle is also the scene of a ghost story grounded in real historical events. In 1648, during the so-called 'Second Civil War' which saw many Royalist uprisings against Parliamentarian rule in the east of England, the Royalist rector of Uffington, Dr Michael Hudson, seized and held the castle for the king with a garrison of fifteen men. Parliamentarian soldiers led by Colonel Waite besieged and eventually breached the castle. Hudson fled to the roof, from which he was thrown by the Parliamentarians, but managed to cling to a ledge or gargoyle. The soldiers hacked off his hands and Hudson fell into the moat, but managed to swim to the other side before he was finally killed by a servant of the rector of Castor.[49] The tradition that the ghost of Dr Hudson still haunted Woodcroft was already current in John Clare's time, and in the 1940s it was reported that the sound of clashing steel and cries of 'Mercy!' and 'Quarter!' could sometimes be heard at night.[50]

The ghost of Dr Hudson does not seem to have been the only one associated with Woodcroft Castle. In one poem written at Northborough, Clare appears to allude to a belief that the spirit of Cromwell still haunted a locked room of the castle:

The castle barn the stranger passes bye
& the old house which many a pencil drew
Some dim seen paintings triump[h] on the walls
& travellers still the antique rooms admire

---

49   Clare (1996–2003), vol. 5, p. 425n.; Orme (2012), pp. 45–7.
50   Westwood and Simpson (2005), pp. 361–2.

Where my lords parlour still the past recalls
Where cromwell doubtless would from strife retire
The locked up room where superstition sleeps
& cromwells memory in dread mystery keeps.[51]

Garton End

The Garton End ghost

In 1926 stories circulated that a short, dark, hooded figure kept appearing on the lane between Dogsthorpe and Garton End now known as Elmfield Road. Older people and children stayed indoors after dark in case the ghost was seen, while others flocked to the area to try and see the apparition. A man named Charles Johnson gave an account to the *Peterborough Advertiser* on 10 April 1926:

> I first heard about the apparition the week before Easter, and I resolved to fathom it if possible. For several nights running, I walked along the lane with my retriever dog, but nothing happened. Last Friday night I was in the lane, proceeding from Dogsthorpe to Garton End. It would be about ten minutes to ten, and suddenly right in front of me, at about 20 to 30 yards away, appeared a black hooded figure of five feet in height. The hood came right down to the ground, and the figure seemed to be gliding along three or four feet from the footpath. I at once bolted forward, and as I did so the figure glided rapidly away, and seemed to melt through the hedge.[52]

Johnson saw the ghost twice more, and it was popularly rumoured to be the spirit of an old 'rag and bone' woman called Mrs Clements, nicknamed 'One-legged Peggy', who had recently died in the Workhouse.[53]

Helpston

East Well

East Well was a holy well in Helpston parish. Clare recollected 'going to east well on a sunday to drink sugar & water at the spring head',[54] although in his 1825 letter to Joseph Hone he suggested the ritual took place on Whitsunday (Pentecost):

> On Whit sunday the village youth of both sexes used to meet at a Fountain calld 'Eastwell' to drink water as a charm for good luck & a preventive of [*illegible*] this was undoubtedly a roman catholic custom as some of the troughs remain still that betoken it to have been an holy well the initials of names & crosses rudely cut with knives are still visible … a pond a [little] distant from this spring is still famous for curing many [ills] & people go often on spring mornings to drink it[,] tho the custom of meeting

---

51   Clare (1996–2003), vol. 5, p. 256.
52   Quoted in Stephen Perry (1992) *A Nostalgic Journey through Garton End*, Peterborough, p. 34.
53   Orme (2012), pp. 76–9.
54   John Clare, Peterborough MS B8, p. 128, quoted in Deacon (1983), p. 68.

at the spring on Whitsunday to drink sugar & water has been abolished ever since the inclosure.[55]

Clare is here describing two separate customs, one associated with the sacred pool close to East Well and not connected with any particular day in the year, and the ritual of 'sugar cupping' specific to Whitsunday. Elsewhere, Clare alluded to 'round oak', a hollow tree next to the spring which was cut down during the enclosure of the village. East Well supposedly never ran dry, and its water was said to be especially effective for eye troubles. The site became known as 'Golden Drop', owing to the sugar cupping practised there.[56]

Will o'the wisps

Clare seems to have had a particular terror of will o'the wisps, and they are mentioned several times in his autobiographical writings. He was never convinced that they could be explained away as natural phenomena, in spite of his more general scepticism about ghosts. However, on one occasion when he was out in Helpston trying to spot a ghost, Clare and his companion witnessed something they had not expected:

> There had been a great upstir in the town about the appearance of the ghost of an old woman who had been recently drownd in a well – it was said to appear at the bottom of neighbour Billings close in a large white winding dress and the noise excited the curiosity of myself and my neighbour to go out several nights together to see if the ghost would be kind enough to appear to us and mend our broken faith in its existance but nothing came[.] on our return we saw a light in the north east over eastwell green and I thought at first that it was a bright meeter[.] It presently became larger and seemd like a light in a window[.] it then moved and dancd up and down and then glided onwards as if a man was riding on hors back at full speed with a lanthorn light[.] soon after this we discoverd another rising in the south east on 'dead moor'[.] they was about a furlong asunder at first and as if the other saw it danced away as if to join it which it soon did and after dancing together a sort of reel as it were – it chaced away to its former station and the other followd it like things at play[;] and after suddenly overtaking it they mingled into one in a moment or else one disapeard and sunk in the ground[.] we stood wondering and gazing for a while at the odd phenomenon and then left the will o wisp dancing to hunt for a companion as it chose.[57]

Clare noted that 'I heard the old alewife at the Exeters arms behind the church (Mrs Nottingham) often say she has seen from one of her chamber windows as many as fifteen together dancing in and out in a company as if dancing reels and dances on east well moor'.[58]

---

55   Quoted in Deacon (1983), pp. 284–5.
56   Clare (1996–2003), vol. 5, p. 417n.
57   Clare (2002), p. 251.
58   Clare (2002), p. 252.

Langley Bush

Until its destruction in 1823, Langley Bush was a local landmark and a seasonal meeting place for the gipsies, with whom John Clare spent much time learning folk songs. However, the bush was also significant because it marked the traditional meeting place of the Hundred Court of the Double Hundred of Nassaburgh. The bush may have been chosen as a meeting place because the Abbot did not permit the court to meet in Peterborough. A similar situation obtained in Bury St Edmunds, where the court of Thingoe Hundred had to meet outside the town owing to the Abbot's refusal to countenance any jurisdiction other than his own.[59] However, it is also possible that the bush marked the ancient gathering place of a 'thing', an Anglo-Saxon open-air public assembly. Clare recorded the destruction of Langley Bush in his journal on 29 September 1824: 'last year Langly bush was destroyd[,] an old white thorn that had stood for more then a century full of fame[.] the Gipseys Shepherds & Herd men all had their tales of its history & it will be long ere its memory is forgotten.'[60] Sadly, other than some mentions of the bush by Clare, those stories have now all been forgotten.

Longthorpe

The wall paintings of Longthorpe Tower

Longthorpe Tower, a fourteenth-century manor house in the care of English Heritage, is famous the world over for its collection of wall paintings, which are unique in northern Europe as a complete collection of late medieval domestic (rather than ecclesiastical) wall paintings. The paintings were rediscovered in 1945, and according to one scholar, 'They defy every reduction, whether to any one text, any one tradition of ideas, or any one culture.' However, the paintings represent a fusion of ideas from the Christian west and Islamic east and reference stories from as far afield as India.[61] Among the most prominent images is a king standing behind a wheel on which are a spider, a boar with pricked ears, a monkey about to eat something from his hand, a cock, and a large bird (probably an eagle or vulture). This was interpreted by Audrey Baker as the 'wheel of the five senses', with the spider representing touch, the boar hearing, the monkey taste, the cock sight and the bird smell. The image is derived from the medieval author Thomas of Cantimpré, with the exception that Cantimpré's lynx is replaced at Longthorpe, uniquely, by the cock as a symbol of sight.[62]

59 Francis Young (2016b) *The Abbey of Bury St Edmunds: History, Legacy and Discovery.* Norwich: Lasse Press, p. 139.
60 Clare (2002), p. 179.
61 Bee Yun (2015) 'The representation of an Indian prince in the Great Chamber of Longthorpe Tower and the intercultural transfer of political ideas in the Middle Ages', *Notes in the History of Art,* 34, pp. 1–6, at p. 6.
62 Edward Clive-Rouse and Audrey Baker (1955) 'The wall-paintings at Longthorpe Tower, near Peterborough', *Archaeologia,* 116, pp. 1–57, at pp. 44–5. For an alternative interpretation of the wheel see Bee Yun (2007) 'A visual mirror of princes: the wheel on the mural of Longthorpe Tower', *Journal of the Warburg and Courtauld Institutes,* 70, pp. 1–32.

Figure 26 The 'wheel of the senses' as depicted in Longthorpe Tower. Photograph by the author.

One theme of the Longthorpe paintings which hints at the stories that may have been enjoyed and told by the tower's inhabitants is depicted next to the visitors' entrance, and is a representation of the Three Living and Three Dead,[63] a popular story depicted in a number of churches (including at nearby Peakirk) but here uniquely portrayed on the walls of a secular building.[64] The Three Living and Three Dead is the tale of three kings who, when out hunting, are confronted by three ghastly revenants who represent their own future corpses and warn them of mortality. In an ecclesiastical context it is clear that the story served as a *memento mori* (reminder of mortality) and a stimulus to repentance, but the appearance of the story in the secular context of Longthorpe Tower points to the other function played by such stories, as entertainment. Catherine Belsey has argued that stories like the Three Living and Three Dead lay at the root of a late medieval tradition of macabre 'winter's tales' which eventually produced the modern ghost story, although the ghosts of medieval tales are not diaphanous spectres but rather revenants, gory walking corpses in an advanced stage of decomposition.

---

63 Clive-Rouse and Baker (1955), pp. 41–2.
64 Catherine Belsey (2010) 'Shakespeare's sad tale for winter: Hamlet and the tradition of fireside ghost stories', *Shakespeare Quarterly*, 61, pp. 1–27, at p. 12. Belsey notes that the Longthorpe depiction was copied from a psalter.

Figure 27 The three dead kings as depicted in Longthorpe Tower. Photograph by the author.

Holywell

Peterborough's most important surviving holy well is located just south-west of Longthorpe in what was once the separate hamlet of Holywell, a name attested in the Middle Ages, although historical evidence of pilgrimage to the site is lacking. There is no shortage of folklore about the well site, although much of this seems to have been invented, and originates from an anonymous story, 'The Knight of the Red Cross, a tale of the 12th century' published in Peterborough around 1850 in a collection of prose and poetry.[65] Here the well is called 'St Cloud's well' and associated with a hermit called St Cloud. The well is now somewhat overgrown, but features a grotto (now covered with an iron grille) and a pool for the outflow in front of it.

St Cloud (Clodoaldus) was a sixth-century Frankish prince who became a hermit for a time, but there is no evidence whatsoever for a cult of St Cloud in England at any time. However, a Somerset village, Temple Cloud, combines the name with an allusion to the Knights Templar (knights of the red cross), and may have given rise to a connection between St Cloud and crusaders in a Victorian author's mind.[66] It seems unlikely that the name 'St Cloud's well' is any older than the nineteenth century, and the suggestion that St Cloud was in fact St Botolph, mentioned by R. B. Parish,[67] is unsupported by any evidence and does not explain how St Botolph came to be so misnamed. John Morton appears to be referring to this well when he alludes to 'a Ditch or Gutter carrying down a small Spring betwixt Longthorp Common and a little Grove',[68] but makes no mention of a grotto or pool, which he would surely have recorded. In around 1720 A. J. Bridges

Figure 28 The overgrown grotto, outflow and pool of Holywell spring at Longthorpe. Photograph by the author.

65 A second edition of *Wild Flowers Gathered: Original pieces, in prose and rhyme* (Peterborough, 1850) can be found in the British Library catalogue, 11644.a.52, but it is unclear when it was first published.
66 I am grateful to Amanda Gryspeerdt for this suggestion.
67 R. B. Parish (2002) 'The Holy Well, or St Cloud's Well, at Longthorpe Park near Peterborough', *Living Spring Journal*, 2 (November), people.bath.ac.uk/liskmj/living-spring/journal/issue2/dipping/rparlon1. htm, accessed 5 January 2017. On this well see also Beeby Thompson (1913) 'Peculiarities of waters and wells', *Journal of the Northamptonshire Natural History Society and Field Club*, 17, pp. 101–15.
68 Morton (1712), p. 152.

reported that 'water rises in a rock or grotto in the park [i.e. Thorpe Park] at some distance from the house'.[69] It seems likely that the grotto and pool are an eighteenth-century folly constructed around the spring by the St John family of Thorpe Park.

Both the spring and the name Holywell are ancient, however, and show that this place was indeed a holy well,[70] although to whom it was dedicated and how it was venerated in the Middle Ages remains unknown. It is just possible that the nineteenth-century story of a knight coming to visit a hermit here was based on an oral tradition preserving a garbled version of the tale of St Wulfade and St Rufinus, in which Wulfade finds St Chad at a holy well (could 'Cloud' be a garbling of Chad?). The ballad reproduced in the windows of the Minster cloister (see Chapter 1) does not give a location for St Chad's well, but it would have made sense for the monks to identify it with a nearby well owned by the abbey in order to direct pilgrims to it. Indeed, the tradition reported by Gunton that Chad concealed Wulfade's heart in the Laurel Yard well in the cloister suggests that the monks were already making efforts to link St Chad with Peterborough sites (see Chapter 1). However, until archaeological evidence of medieval pilgrimage at Holywell is uncovered, a connection between the well and the cult of St Chad must remain purely in the realm of speculation.

Maxey

Ghosts, hobgoblins and will o'the wisps

Maxey is a remote village located on the banks of the Welland north of Helpston. When he was working for Francis Gregory, landlord of the Blue Bell in Helpston, the young John Clare had to walk there to fetch flour. Clare recalled that 'in these journeys I had haunted spots to pass & as the often heard tales of ghosts & hobgoblins had made me very fearful to pass such places at night it being often nearly dark ere I got there I usd to employ my mind as well as I was able to put these out of my head'. According to Clare, it was the stories he made up to distract himself that developed his storytelling ability, as well as giving him a lifelong habit of talking to himself.[71]

Clare recalled encountering will o'the wisps in the bleak, flat landscape between Helpston and Maxey, on one occasion on Nunton Bridge over Maxey Cut, marking the boundary between the two parishes:

> I was terribly frighted on seeing a will owisp for the first time and tho my fears grew less by custom for there are crowds about our fenny flats yet I never coud take them on credit of philos[oph]y as natural phenomenons at night time but always had a suspicion of somthing supernatural belonging to them ... in this november month they are often out in the dark misty nights – on 'Rotten Moor' 'Dead Moor' Eastwell moor – Banton green end Lolham Briggs Rine dyke furlong and many other places in the lordship[.] I

---

69   Quoted on the public information board at Holywell.

70   The suggestion on the public information board at Holywell that the name of the site means 'hollow well' or 'well in the hollow' and has no religious connotations seems unlikely and is unsupported by toponymic evidence, as there are many places in England called Holywell.

71   Quoted in Deacon (1983), pp. 48–9.

have my self seen them on most of these spots – one dark night I was coming accross the new parks when a sudden light wild and pale appeared all round me on my left hand for a hundred yards or more accompany[i]ed by a crackling noise like that of peas straw burning[.] I stood looking for a minute or so and felt rather alarmed when darkness came round me again and one of the dancing jack a la[n]thens was whisking away in the distance which caused the odd luminous light around me – crossing the meadow one dark sunday night I saw when coming over the Nunton bright a light like a lanthorn standing on the wall of the other bridge[.] I kept my eyes on it for awhile and hastened to come up to it – but ere I got half over the meadow it suddenly fell and tumbled into the stream – but when I got on the bridge I looked down it and saw the will o whi[s]p vapour like a light in a bladder whisking along close to the water as if swimming along its surface but what supprised me was that it was going contrary to the stream.[72]

Northborough

Northborough Castle

John Clare 'flitted' with his family from Helpston to the neighbouring parish of Northborough in 1832, and the place is frequently mentioned in his poetry. 'Northborough Castle', really a fortified fourteenth-century manor house, was famous locally as the place to which Elizabeth Cromwell, wife of Oliver, retired after the Restoration of the Monarchy in 1660. There was also a local tradition in Northborough that Oliver Cromwell was buried there, and in 1854 a Mr Markland wrote to the journal *Notes and Queries* to report that 'it was common knowledge locally' that Cromwell's body had been secretly buried in an unmarked grave in the village.[73]

Orton Longueville (see also Bottlebridge)

The disembowelled knight of Orton Longueville

Hidden behind the stalls on the north side of the chancel of Orton Longueville church is the recumbent effigy of a medieval knight, tentatively identified by the church as Sir John de Longueville, who died before 1265. However, in previous centuries the people of Orton Longueville developed their own legend about the knight, whose effigy has one curious feature. The knight's hands are joined in prayer, and around his left wrist is what appears to be a ring of cloth. However, local people saw a resemblance to intestines, and told this story: 'A Lord Longueville, who, in fighting with the Danes near this place, received a wound in the abdomen, so that his bowels fell out; but wrapping them round the wrist of his left arm, he continued the combat with his right hand till he had killed the Danish King, and soon after fell himself.'[74] The obvious anachronism in the story is that a Norman de Longueville could not have fought the Danes, but the Danes often served as all-purpose antagonists in folklore about ancient battles and fortifications, so it is not surprising to find them here. However, it remains unclear what the object around

72   Clare (2002), pp. 45–6.
73   Codd (2009), p. 26.
74   Saunders (1888), p. 299.

Figure 29 Effigy of a 'disembowelled' knight, Holy Trinity church, Orton Longueville. Photograph by the author.

the knight's left wrist really is, so the legend may provide as good an explanation as any.

Jack Raveley

Jack Raveley was a local Peterborough eccentric of the mid-nineteenth century who gave his name to a landscape feature in Orton Longueville. His mysterious arrival was described by W. H. Saunders:

A gravelly shallow, near Overton Longueville, which deepens into a hole is known as 'Raveley's Hole,' and is familiar to anglers and bathers. Somewhere between the decade of 1840 and 1850 there went to Peterborough a tall, thin, lanky, half-silly youth, about the age of 16. He had no occupation, and no means of subsistance. He could give no account of himself, not even of his name. If he had any parents ... he did not know them, and they were ignorant of him. In place of a better, the public of Peterborough awarded him the name of 'Jack' for a christian name, and as he was supposed to have come from the village of Raveley he had that added for a surname .... He settled down very comfortably under the name chosen for him by the popular voice of Peterborough, and he answered to it readily. His oddities and eccentricities made him familiar in the town and a butt for the wit and humour of young men. He was accustomed to account for any imperfections in the upper story by declaring that going one day a little too near the Town Mill, which at that time stood upon the Thorpe-road, nearly opposite the present Gaol, one of the sails struck him on the head, and ever afterwards his understanding became cloudy .... Amongst his many peculiarities he is said to have been an exceedingly swift runner, and was a constant competitor in foot races.[75]

---

75   Saunders (1888), pp. 230–2.

However, it was the manner of Jack Raveley's death that gave 'Raveley's Hole' its name:

> [D]uring the summer he was accustomed to resort to the Nene for a bathe. One day he entered the water at the gravelly shallow, and although unable to swim, he waded across to the opposite meadow, and, after disporting himself for a time, proceeded to re-cross the stream. But he failed to recognise the exact spot, and instead of keeping to the shallow water he was soon plunging in the deep hole close by. Assistance not being at hand he was drowned. The body was drawn out of on the Huntingdonshire side of the river, and he was buried in Woodstone Church-yard at the expense of the parish, and entred in the register by the name accorded to him by the popular voice of the residents of the city.[76]

Paston

Spectres in Paston churchyard

In 1911 the *Peterborough Advertiser* recounted a story from Paston associated with the custom of 'watching' in churchyards on St Mark's Eve (24 April). The story originated with a Mrs Whittam who was living in Thorney in 1911 but remembered an incident from her childhood in Paston:

> Years ago when Mr. Pratt was rector of Paston,

Figure 30
Paston churchyard. Photograph by the author.

---

76   Saunders (1888), p. 233.

there was a woman who lived at Werrington, and she was accustomed to go and wash[77] at Paston Rectory. It was customary to commence washing very early in the morning. One moonlight (*sic.*) night this woman, under the impression that it was early morning – for few cottages possessed a clock in those days – reached Paston Churchyard at midnight. She had to pass through the churchyard to reach the Rectory, there being then a field intervening between the churchyard and the Rectory. But when she reached the church-yard-gate she found the graveyard full of funerals and weddings. She was very frightened and ran through them and into the adjoining field to the Rectory. There of course the house was locked up, but she awoke the servants. Next morning she told Mr. Pratt of her strange experience of the previous midnight, but he only smiled and said, 'Yes, yes; of course, it was St. Mark's Eve.'[78]

Peakirk

St Pega of Peakirk

According to legend, Peakirk was founded as a monastery in the eighth century by St Pega (d. 719), the sister of St Guthlac of Crowland, which would seem to be supported by place name evidence but is not otherwise attested except in much later medieval sources.[79] Known locally as St Pee, Pega is a somewhat obscure figure who arranged the burial of her brother Guthlac and subsequently made a pilgrimage to Rome, where she died. In the early Middle Ages pilgrimages to far-flung places such as Rome and Jerusalem were considered heroic and often resulted in the death of the traveller, serving to some extent as a substitute for martyrdom. Furthermore, the holy sites were of such potency that prayer there was regarded as especially powerful, and Pega was one of few English 'pilgrim saints'.[80] Pega helped to establish Guthlac's cult at Crowland, and at his burial healed a blind man with salt consecrated by Guthlac before his death.[81] According to one legend, Pega caused all the bells in Rome to ring miraculously for an hour before making a speech in which she declared her sanctity.[82]

In the eleventh century the monastery at Peakirk (which, like Peterborough, was re-founded after the Danish destruction) became embroiled in a dispute with Peterborough Abbey which was decided by King Harthacnut in 1048 in favour of Peterborough. The monastery at Peakirk ceased to have any independent existence and Peterborough neglected the site until 1477 when Abbot John Wysbech built a chapel at 'Payland' (the so-called

---

77 'Wash', i.e. do the laundry.
78 'A weird local custom!', *Peterborough Advertiser*, 17 May 1911, newspaper cutting in CUL, Lib.5.89. 520–1, p. 265.
79 F. M. Stenton (1943) 'The historical bearing of place-name studies: the place of women in Anglo-Saxon Society', *Transactions of the Royal Historical Society*, 25, pp. 1–13, at p. 9n. concluded that 'there is no reason to doubt' Peakirk was named after Pega. For a discussion of the issue see Avril Lumley Prior (2008) 'Fact and/or folklore? The case for St Pega of Peakirk', *Northamptonshire Past and Present*, 61, pp. 7–16.
80 Patricia A. Halpin (1997) 'Anglo-Saxon women and pilgrimage', pp. 97–122 in Christopher Harper-Bill (ed.), *Anglo-Norman Studies, 19: Proceedings of the Battle Conference 1996*, Woodbridge: Boydell Press, at p. 98.
81 Halpin (1997), p. 107.
82 Story (1883), p. 46.

Figure 31 St Pega
boarding a ship to travel
to Rome, from a stained
glass window in the
south aisle of St John's
church, Peterborough.
Photograph by the
author.

Figure 31 St Pega boarding a ship to travel to Rome, from a stained glass window in the south aisle of St John's church, Peterborough. Photograph by the author.

Hermitage).[83] Until 1995 the Hermitage was occupied by a group of Anglican nuns, the Community of the Holy Family, who believed that St Pega was associated with swans.[84] It seems likely that this is a recent tradition, perhaps derived from Peakirk's fame as a sanctuary for waterfowl in the twentieth century,[85] or else from the modern stained glass window in Peakirk parish church commemorating Lilian Mary James (1950) showing St Pega surrounded by swans.

Set into a recess inside the parish church is a wooden reliquary that is supposed to contain St Pega's heart,[86] but it seems likely that this is a post-Reformation tradition which, like the stories about St Kyneburgha at Castor, grew up as a result of local pride in a unique dedication to a local saint. The church also contains a wall painting depicting the legend of the Three Living and Three Dead (see Longthorpe).

---

83 See Gunton (1686), pp. 252–4.
84 See umilta.net/pega.html, accessed 3 January 2017.
85 The association between St Pega and wildfowl is suggested, without evidence, by Martin Palmer and Nigel Palmer (2000) *The Spiritual Traveller: England, Scotland, Wales: The guide to sacred sites and pilgrim routes in Britain,* Mahwah, N.J.: HiddenSpring, p. 128.
86 Bunch and Liquorice (1990), p. 26.

Stanground

The Stoneground Ghost Tales

Edmund Gill Swain (1861–1938) was rector of Stanground between 1905 and 1916 and a friend of M. R. James, the celebrated antiquary and writer of ghost stories, whom Swain tried to imitate in his collection of supernatural stories *The Stoneground Ghost Tales* (1912). Set in the village of 'Stoneground' (which is obviously Stanground) and featuring its rector the Reverend Roland Batchel (who is obviously Swain himself), *The Stoneground Ghost Tales* may preserve elements of Stanground folklore, with many of them being grounded in the village's genuine history. However, since no study of the folklore of Stanground exists, the relationship between Swain's stories and actual folklore remains speculative.

The story 'The man with the roller' features a photograph taken in the rectory garden which, when developed, reveals the image of a man pushing a roller over the lawn. This turns out to be the unquiet ghost of a seventeenth-century murderer who buried his victim in the garden and attempted to cover his tracks by obsessively pushing a roller over the spot.[87] In 'The Richpins' the ghost of an escaped French prisoner from the camp at Norman Cross, Jules Richepin, haunts 'Frenchman's Meadow', which still exists on the south side of the Nene between the village and Stanground sluice and is described with some precision by Swain:

> It was on the edge of what is known locally as 'high land'; and although its elevation was not great, one could stand in the meadow and look sea-wards over many miles of flat country, once a waste of brackish water, now a great chess-board of fertile fields bounded by straight dykes of glistening water. The point of view derived another interest from looking down upon a long straight bank which disappeared into the horizon many miles away, and might have been taken for a great railway embankment of which no use

Figure 32 The old rectory at Stanground, home of E. G. Swain and his fictional counterpart, Mr Batchel. Photograph by the author.

---

87   Swain (2009), pp. 7–17.

Figure 33 Stanground sluice, the site of the sluice-keeper's cottage in E. G. Swain's story 'The Richpins'. Photograph by the author.

was made. It was, in fact, one of the great works of the Dutch Engineers in the time of Charles I, and it separated the river basin from a large drained area called the 'Middle Level', some six feet below it. In this embankment, not two hundred yards below 'Frenchman's Meadow', was one of the huge water gates which admitted traffic through a sluice, into the lower level, and the picturesque thatched cottage of the sluice-keeper formed a pleasing addition to the landscape.[88]

In the story, the ghost of Jules Richepin is haunting the meadow because, after his escape, he hid in the rafters of the sluice-keeper's cottage and starved to death there; at the end of the story his body is found and given a Christian burial, bringing the haunting to an end. No 'picturesque thatched cottage' now stands by the sluice but a modern house stands on the site. 'The Richpins' is an especially interesting story from the point of view of Stanground's history because it seems to have been inspired by the fact that several of Swain's parishioners had French surnames and were the descendants of Norman Cross prisoners who, on their release in 1814, married local women rather than returning home to France:

---

88   Swain (2009), p. 38.

Amongst the household treasures of the old inhabitants are invariably found French knickknacks: there are pieces of French furniture in what is called 'the room' of many houses. A certain ten-acre field is called the 'Frenchman's meadow'. Upon the voters' lists hanging at the church door are to be found French names, often corrupted, and boys who run about the streets can be heard shrieking to each other such names as Bunnum,[89] Dangibow,[90] Planchey, and so on.[91]

Swain certainly did not make this up, and tombstones with French names on them can be seen in several local churchyards. A key plot element of the story is the physical resemblance of a man in the village, Thomas Richpin, to the spectre, so much so that the ghost is mistaken for Mr Richpin. Richpin retains a vague and fading memory of his French ancestors, but Swain emphasises the extent to which the inhabitants of early twentieth-century Stanground had already forgotten their French forebears.

In the story 'The rockery', Mr Batchel and his gardener foolishly remove a stake they find in the rectory's rockery ominously inscribed 'Move not this stake', which turns out to have been driven into the body of a suicide buried there in chains in 1702. The ghost of the man rises and causes havoc in the local area.[92] In 'The place of safety', Batchel witnesses the ghosts of a sixteenth-century vicar and parishioners loading the church plate onto a barge in 1552 in order to save it from confiscation by Edward VI's commissioners,[93] while 'The kirk spook' is a humorous story about a parish clerk who encounters and then releases a ghost trapped in Stanground church.[94]

Charley Strickson

The Stanground shoemaker Charley Strickson (c. 1787–1857) was renowned for being astonishingly thin and unable to look at anyone or anything fat:

Although a shoemaker by trade he came of noble stock – at least so he boasted. His chief peculiarity was an abhorrence of all that tended to embonpoint that it is said he would seek to pass by on the other side any portly resident, whilst he was never to be seen on the Long Causeway at Peterborough when the fat stock fair was being held there. It may thus be imagined he was thin, so thin indeed that his tailor made special bargains with him, the boys of the place made fun at him, and the ordinary passer-by turned his head to take a second glance. Amongst his eccentricities especially to be noticed was a peculiarity in his dress. No ordinary attire would do, and he would consequently be seen dressed in a cutaway coat, and a pair of black trowsers which had shrunk up to within a few inches of his knees, leaving his spindle legs poking through and terminating in a pair of low shoes and buckles. On his head was a beaver top hat – he would wear no other – and he stood five feet eight inches in his boots .... No one

---

89   A corruption of Bonhomme.
90   A corruption of D'Angebois.
91   Swain (2009), p. 28.
92   Swain (2009), pp. 72–84.
93   Swain (2009), pp. 101–18.
94   Swain (2009), pp. 119–26.

particularly knew his antecedents, had not his earnest asseverations as to a high born genealogy been to the contrary. It mattered little to his patrons; he was a good cobbler, and was a first-class shoemaker; his charges were reasonable, and that for ordinary purposes was sufficient, especially as he had been the family workman, possibly, for years. Although in his rounds he wore his cutaway coat, his beaver hat, and his black trowsers, and had high notions of his antecedents, yet he was never above his trade, and his shoemaking apron always hid his waistcoat. A great peculiarity in it was a hole at the breast, which, however often it was replenished with a new one, would assuredly make its appearance. This, it subsequently transpired, was not by accident but was purposely cut by our hero himself, and was regarded by Charley with a superstitious reverence. Though noticed by all, for years the why and wherefore remained a profound secret. It was rumoured that it was to perpetuate the assassination of an ancestor of some two or three generations back! Winter or summer the eccentric shoemaker would be found with a flower in his button hole, and more frequently than not in summer it would be a common nettle, which he would carefully explain, "Stroke it the right way, sir, and it won't sting, neither will a Strickson." For many years he followed an old custom of retailing frumenty (or firmity) on Good Friday mornings. The receipt for this ancient "mess of pottage" he always declared had descended through his family for generations, which he alone considered indisputable testimony of its quality.

In 1848 Strickson's wife accidentally drowned in a drain at Newark, and Strickson himself died about nine years later.[95]

Thornhaugh

Sacrewell

Located in the parish of Thornhaugh, Sacrewell Farm was established as a working educational farm by Mary Abbott in 1964 and is open to visitors throughout the year. John Morton called the place 'Saker-Well' in 1712,[96] and the editors of the *Victoria County History* of Northamptonshire concluded in 1906 that the place was named after a 'sacred well' that rose close to Sacrewell Lodge.[97] This etymology seems highly likely, although the form 'Sacrewell' is rare in comparison with the more common 'Holywell' (with its variants Hollywell and Halliwell) as a reminder that a place was once associated with a holy well. No record survives of the holy well itself, and the name of the place is all the evidence there is that Sacrewell was ever a place of pilgrimage or popular religious devotion.

95   Saunders (1888), pp. 228–30.
96   Morton (1712), p. 532.
97   R. M. Serjeantson and William Ryland D. Adkins (eds) (1906) *The Victoria History of the County of Northampton*, London: Archibald Constable, vol. 2, p. 530.

Figure 34
Sacrewell mill pond.
Photograph by the
author.

Upton

A haunted cottage

On 13 March 1920 the *Peterborough Advertiser* reported that a cottage at Upton occupied by the family of John Macro, a tree-feller employed by the Fitzwilliam family of Milton Hall, had been haunted by unexplained sounds in the night and the apparition of a woman in white, as well as a creature with a tail that was about 15 inches long and made a sound like a car starting. The only thing that would prevent the apparitions was for the family to sleep with the lights on. The *Advertiser* also reported that previous occupants had fled the house on account of the apparitions and that the rector of Upton had spent the night there in the hope of seeing the ghost. These latter two claims were furiously refuted in the *Advertiser*'s 20 March edition in a letter from the rector, who discouraged ghost-seekers from visiting the village.[98]

Wansford

Wansford-in-England

One of the best-known folktales of the Peterborough area is associated with Wansford Bridge, the impressive structure (in its present form dating from 1796) that used to carry the Great North Road over the River Nene. Consequently half of Wansford was traditionally in Huntingdonshire and the other half in Northamptonshire, and it remains the case that only the northern part of Wansford is now in Peterborough Unitary Authority. The village's nickname 'Wansford-in-England' derives from a tale

---

98   Orme (2012), pp. 81–2.

Figure 35 Wansford Bridge. Photograph by the author.

that first appeared in print in 1638 in a series of comic poems entitled *Drunken Barnaby's Four Journeys to the North of England*:

> On a Hay-cock sleeping soundly,
> Th'River rose, and took me roundly,
> Down the Current: People cry'd,
> Sleeping down the Stream I hy'd:
> *Where away*, quoth they, *from Greenland*?
> No, from Wansforth-brigs in England.

In 1712 John Morton made clear that the story concerned a man who fell asleep on a haycock and was carried away from Wansford, presumably downstream in the direction of Peterborough:

> [A] Man, who, as he was fast asleep on a little Haycock in a Meadow on the Nyne, nigh Wansford, never dreaming either of Floods or Rain, was carry'd off by one of these Floods with his Haycock under him. The poor Man at length awakes, and looks about him with all the Surprize imaginable. He had laid down to sleep on a Haycock, in a dry Meadow nigh Wansford; but finds himself afloat in the midst of Waters, for ought he knew in the wide Ocean. As their Story goes, one espying him in this Condition, calls to him, and enquires where he lived: The poor Fellow, in a piteous Tone, reply'd, At Wansford in England.[99]

---

99   Quoted in Westwood and Simpson (2005), pp. 368–9.

Figure 36 The Haycock Inn, Wansford. Photograph by the author.

Figure 37 (below) The legend of Wansford Bridge as depicted on the side of the Haycock Inn. Photograph by the author.

Later versions of the story (including the painted depiction on the front of the Haycock Inn) have the man being carried *to* rather than away from Wansford, and shouting up to a man on Wansford Bridge who informs him he is at Wansford, in England. The story would seem to be a joke at the expense of rustics whose view of the world was so parochial that they thought flood-waters might carry them away from England. The Haycock Inn, one of the great coaching inns of the Great North Road, is named after the Wansford legend.[100]

Woodston

The woman in black

One Peterborough ghost sighting that seems to have passed into folk tradition was the 'woman in black', first sighted in Woodston in 1908. In October 1973 the *Peterborough Citizen and Advertiser* tried to uncover the truth about the story, and interviewed an eyewitness, Ada Lilly, who claimed the ghost was that of a poor woman from Belsize Avenue, then renowned as the poorest and roughest area of Woodston and nicknamed 'the Klondike', who vowed to return after death to ensure her children were not neglected. The figure of a woman in black was subsequently sighted in Woodston

---

100 D. Glenn, 'Peterborough inn signs and their strange origin', 27 November 1903, newspaper cutting in CUL, Lib.5.89.520–1, p. 58.

churchyard and in the lane running along the west side of the parish church. One woman fainted on seeing the apparition, and a group of six young men arrived armed with wooden stakes to 'lay' the ghost, presumably intending to drive them into the ground where the woman was buried to prevent her 'walking'. When the woman's children moved away the hauntings stopped, but at the height of the hauntings the parish council reportedly put up notices to warn people of the ghost.[101]

Yaxley

A large part of the northern portion of the ancient parish of Yaxley now falls within Peterborough Unitary Authority, and some of the new development of Hampton is in what used to be Yaxley. Although the village of Yaxley itself falls outside the Peterborough region, its folklore is included here because part of the ancient parish is within the boundaries.

Libations to the dead

The *Huntingdonshire, Bedfordshire and Peterborough Weekly Gazette* of 13 January 1816 reported a strange discovery in Yaxley churchyard: 'The sexton of Yaxley in digging a grave broke through the side of a coffin and out fell a glass bottle which, from the inscription on the gravestone, had been there for 27 years. The cork was drawn, and the contents proved to be excellent Old Stingo.'[102] This curious find is reminiscent of an archaeological discovery made in the Minster precincts, where a small glass bowl was recovered from a seventh-century Christian burial associated with the original monastery of Medeshamstede. Christian burial was supposed to do away with pagan 'grave goods', but as these discoveries a thousand years apart show, the idea of 'libations' – giving drink to the dead – has proved a hard one to eradicate.

A wonder of Huntingdonshire

An old rhyme described 'Yaxley stone mill' as one of 'the three wonders of Huntingdonshire', and C. F. Tebbutt noted that when a windmill on the south side of the road between Yaxley and Norman Cross was pulled down in 1935, 'it was found to have foundation courses of Barnack stone arranged in such fashion as to show that on them once stood the most ancient type of post mill. It also had the rare feature of a stone walled cellar, from which, tradition said, an underground passage ran to Yaxley Church.'[103]

A mysterious heart

Yaxley church contains a medieval box that once contained a human heart, which can still be seen today in a recess in the north transept covered by glass. The discovery was made in 1842, when:

---

101 For a full account of the haunting see Orme (2012), p. 75.
102 C. F. Tebbutt (1952) *Huntingdonshire Folklore*, St Ives: privately published, p. 4.
103 Tebbutt (1952), p. 15.

[A] stone carved with two hands holding a heart was removed from a wall in the north transept. Behind it a cylindrical wooden box, 4 ½ inches (9cms) by 4 inches (8cm) was found. The box contained a heart, but as soon as this was exposed to the air it disintegrated. There was, and is, nothing left to identify the heart; but it is believed to have belonged to William de Yaxley, Abbot of Thorney 1261 to 1293, who directed that his body was to be buried in the Abbey but his heart at Yaxley'.[104]

A sacrilegious baptism

Gunton made a detailed record of all the damage done to Peterborough Minster by Cromwell's soldiers in 1643, and took the opportunity to add a story about Yaxley church as well:

> And now I am engaged in telling the story of their impiety and profaneness at Peterburgh, 'twill be no great excursion to step out to Yaxley a neighbouring Town, and mention one thing done there. Which was This: on the 10th of June 1643. some of Captain Beaumont's Souldiers coming thither, They break open the Church doors, piss in the Font, and then baptize a Horse and a Mare, using the solemn words of Baptism, and signing them with the sign of the Cross.

This was not an act of random sacrilege but a directed criticism of what many Puritans saw as an abuse in the Church of England, the signing with the cross in baptism. For Puritans, baptism was nothing more than a symbolic act, whereas 'high churchmen' regarded baptism as a sacrament that effected a real change in the person baptised, sealed by the sign of the cross. By baptising a horse and a mare the soldiers were showing their contempt for the official doctrine of the Church of England.

May Day revived

Since 2013, as part of the Yaxley Festival, the village has seen a revival of its May Day procession, which has been embellished with the addition of 'Jack-in-the-Green' and two attendant characters, the snake-charmer Sap-engro and Copperface.[105] Jack-in-the-Green is a performer completely covered in foliage and is traditionally connected with the 'green man' often seen as a decoration on medieval churches. Although there is no evidence that Jack-in-the-Green was part of the village's original May Day celebrations, the Yaxley celebrations show that folk customs have a life of their own that cannot be constrained by a fixed and unchanging tradition.

---

104 Bunch and Liquorice (1990), p. 44.
105 'Preview: three-day Yaxley Festival celebration', *Peterborough Telegraph*, online edition, 15 May 2014, peterboroughtoday.co.uk/whats-on/arts/preview-three-day-yaxley-festival-celebration-1-6060572, accessed 3 January 2017.

Chapter 4

The Peterborough year

Many of Peterborough's ancient customs are associated with particular days in the calendar, some fixed dates and others 'moveable feasts' such as the days associated with the season of Lent and Easter. Some Peterborough customs are entirely unique – such as ringing the bells of St John's church on 'Wyldbore's Day'. Others are similar to customs elsewhere in the country, but with a distinctive regional twist, such as the Peterborough Plough Monday celebrations. However, a few customs recorded by earlier folklorists were so generic – such as visiting mothers on Mothering Sunday, bonfires on 5 November, and singing 'Good King Wenceslas' on Christmas Eve – that they are not included here. Modern traditions such as Peterborough Cathedral's annual festival in honour of Katharine of Aragon in late January are also omitted, although they are an important part of Peterborough's contemporary calendar. Anyone wishing to compare the customs of Peterborough with similar practices in the rest of England should consult the standard works on the English ritual year, Steve Roud's *The English Year* or *The Stations of the Sun* by Ronald Hutton.[1]

January

1 *New Year's Day*

John Clare wrote that 'The first moon in the new year young men & maids look through a silk hankerchief (that has been drawn through a ring) at [the] New moon & as many moons as each person sees through it [so] many years will they be ere they are married.'[2]

The New Year custom of beer tasting in Peterborough's public houses, reported by Dack, seems to have been more of a confidence trick than anything else:

> Three or four old men, each with a small wooden key or bottle, or even a leather bottle, each holding from two to three pints, and strapped round their waists – one had a funnel as well – used to visit the public houses in the city. Their greeting to the attendant at the bar was: 'Tell the master (or mistress) that the beer-tasters have come'. They were then given a pint of beer in a mug, and after each man had taken a sip the rest was poured through the funnel into one of the receptacles they carried, and off they went to the next house, where the same thing was repeated. No one can remember

---

1   Steve Roud (2006) *The English Year: a month-by-month guide to the nation's customs and festivals, from May Day to Mischief Night*, London: Penguin. Ronald Hutton (1996) *The Stations of the Sun: A history of the ritual year in Britain*, Oxford: Oxford University Press.
2   Quoted in Deacon (1983), p. 286.

by what authority this was done, but if the men were dissatisfied with the beer they threatened to report the landlord; but as nothing was afterwards heard of any report, the landlords were not so particular as to what kind of beer was given; and at last they refused to give any more beer, and the tasters disappeared.[3]

Dack also reported a divination custom for New Year's Day: 'The first thing on New Year's morning, open your Bible and the first verse your finger or thumb touches will betoken what will occur during the year.' Furthermore, 'if a sprig of green is placed in the Bible, the verse on which it lies will foretell the events of the year'. It was considered lucky for a dark-haired man to be the first to enter the house on New Year's Day, with some people arranging this specifically and offering food and drink as an inducement to a suitably dark-haired individual. On leaving the house for the first time on New Year's Day, it was good luck to pick up a piece of gold that had been concealed outside the house.[4]

6 Epiphany

In the late nineteenth century, the confectioners of Peterborough used to raffle iced buns on this day.[5]

7 Old Christmas Day

In September 1752 Great Britain and its colonies switched from the Julian to the Gregorian Calendar, meaning that eleven days of the month disappeared (the gap between the two calendars is now thirteen days). This was deeply unpopular, especially in the countryside where people's awareness of time was highly developed and specific days in the calendar were associated with agricultural events. The celebration of Old Christmas Day was particularly persistent and lasted into the twentieth century in some localities.

Monday after Epiphany (Plough Monday)

See Chapter 2 for an account of the 'Plough witches' associated with this day. The inhabitants of Peterborough's almshouses received a dole of candles on this day, according to the will of a Mr Towers who died in 1711.[6] John Hales, in his account of the old customs of Castor, makes no reference to plough witches but describes a ploughing competition between the men of Castor and Ailsworth:

[A] bell rope was obtained and sticks knotted in it, and about a score lads with a primitive plough to Milton, where other parishes met them, and a trial of strength was indulged in, but the climax was about one o'clock when they returned, and Castor and Ailsworth met at the division of the two parishes, and hooked ploughs together to see

3   Dack (1899), p. 338.
4   Dack (1911), p. 8.
5   Dack (1899), p. 323.
6   Dack (1899), p. 324.

which were the strongest, the women giving great aid in pulling; this generally wound up with a free fight.[7]

In around 1840 a wooden plough kept in the belfry of Castor church, presumably for the Plough Monday festivities, was broken up and burned by workmen in order to dry some plaster.[8] In 1911 Dack reported that 'Only two lots of men were seen in Peterborough this year, the Stores no doubt not encouraging them as the tradesmen did in old times.'[9]

8 *St Pega's Day*

St Pega, foundress of the monastery at Peakirk, died in Rome on this day in 719 and her feast day was celebrated on this date in the Middle Ages.[10]

25 *St Paul's Day*

This is actually the Feast of the Conversion of St Paul, with St Paul's martyrdom being commemorated (along with St Peter's) on 29 June. Dack noted down some weather lore for this day 'From a copy of verses ... to all my worthy Masters and Mistresses, by John Small, Bell-man, Stamford 1850':

Figure 38 St Pega surrounded by swans, from a stained glass window in St Pega's church, Peakirk. Photograph by the author.

If Saint Paul's day be fair and clear,
It doth betide a happy year,

7   CAMUS (2004), p. 349.
8   CAMUS (2004), p. 73.
9   Dack (1911), p. 8.
10   Story (1883), p. 46.

If blustering winds to blow aloft,
Then wars will trouble our realm full oft,
And if by chance to snow or rain,
Then will be dear all sorts of grain.[11]

February

2 *Candlemas Day*

Candlemas Day, or the Feast of the Presentation of Our Lord in the Temple,

> [I]s one of those fateful days when old ladies very carefully observe the weather, for, as the old couplets have it: 'If Candlemas Day be fine and clear, / There will be two winters in one year. / But if Candlemas Day brings clouds and rain, / Winter is gone and will not come again. / When the wind's in the East on Candlemas Day, / There it will stick to the second of May.'[12]

13 *Baulk Valentine*

The night preceding St Valentine's Day featured a local variant of 'knock-down-ginger':

> It is the custom for the night of the 13th February to be called Baulk Valentine, as on this night mischievous people or urchins would give runaway knocks, or ring the bells at various houses. Sometimes a packet or parcel, affixed to a piece of string, was put on the doorstep, a knock given, and the person answering and opening the door would see the parcel and stoop to pick it up; then the lad with the string would jerk it away. Occasionally, these packets were sent by spiteful people, and had pins fixed in them point upward to catch and scratch their hands.[13]

14 *St Valentine's Day*

A St Valentine's Day song was sung by children in Peterborough and its surrounding villages on this day:

> Good morrow Valentine,
> Please to give me your Valentine;
> I'll be yourn, if you'll be mine,
> Please give me a Valentine.

It was also traditional to make 'sweet plum buns', which were given by godfathers and godmothers to their godchildren on the Sunday before and the Sunday after 14 February.[14]

---

11   MS note in the hand of Charles Dack in CUL, Lib.5.89.520–1, p. 212.
12   'Candlemas Couplets', *Peterborough Standard*, 10 February 1912, newspaper cutting in CUL, Lib.5.89.520–1, p. 84.
13   Dack (1899), p. 324.
14   'Curious local customs: Mr. C. Dack's fascinating paper', 12 April 1905, newspaper cutting in CUL,

Shrove Tuesday

St John's church in Peterborough rang its sanctus bell at a quarter to twelve on Shrove Tuesday, which was known as the 'Pancake Bell'.[15] At Castor, in addition to the Pancake Bell being rung at noon, pancakes were thrown out of the windows of the belfry.[16]

It was the custom on Shrove Tuesday to throw stones at cocks. The Constable's Book at Castor for 27 February 1759 notes that the constable claimed a shilling 'For returning a warrant to prevent the Cox being holled at on Shrove Tuesday'.[17]

March

7 *Translation of St Kyneburgha, St Kyneswitha and St Tibba*

In the Middle Ages the removal of the bodies of Kyneburgha and Kyneswitha from Castor to Peterborough, and of Tibba from Ryhall, Staffordshire to Peterborough were cele-brated on this day.[18] The three women were all sisters of King Peada, the founder of Medeshamstede, and all became nuns and abbesses. Although their shrine continued to be visited by pilgrims up to the Reformation, it is doubtful whether the bodies of these saints survived the Danish destruction of Peterborough in the ninth century.[19] Nevertheless, Peada's three sisters were important to Peterbor-ough Abbey because they were its only local saints, and a hymn in honour of the saints was sung on the feast of their translation:

Now let Burgh's church offer the Lord
Praise with St Peter in accord;
Bright shining Kyneburgha, raise
With Kyneswide and Tibba praise.
'Gainst him that dared their bones
  remove

Figure 39 Possible fragment of the tomb-shrine of St Kyneburgha, Castor church.
Photograph by the author.

Lib.5.89.521, p. 80.
15 Dack (1899), p. 325.
16 CAMUS (2004), p. 349.
17 Bunch and Liquorice (1990), p. 4.
18 There is some doubt about whether this feast should be celebrated on 6 or 7 March, with different sources giving both dates; however, the present-day church of St Kyneburgha at Castor celebrates 7 March so I have adopted this date.
19 Gunton (1686) p. 322.

Both king and people tempest drove
That might have shipwrecked; yet the Lord
Commanding soon spread peace abroad.
Now prosper us, blest Trinity,
Together with these sisters three.
Thus God did gloriously provide
From Penda by whom Oswald died
Two roses from the pagan thorn
For Christ did grow, to Christ were sworn.
Now glory to the Trinity,
To Father, Son and Spirit three.[20]

The children of Castor School lay flowers on the remains of the shrine of St Kyneburgha every year on 7 March, although this practice is likely to be a revival of recent date.[21]

15 *Wyldbore's Day*

Matthew Wyldbore (c. 1716–81) was MP for Peterborough between 1768 and 1780, living at a mansion (now demolished) in Westgate. One day Wyldbore was on the common between the city and Peterborough Great Fen when a fog suddenly rose and he was afraid to move in case he fell into a drain or dyke. However, the bells of St John's then began to ring and he found his way home. In his will Wyldbore stipulated that the bells of St John's should be rung on the anniversary of his death (15 March 1781) and that money and entertainment should be given to the bell-ringers, as well as a dole distributed to the poor.[22]

Palm Sunday

It was a local custom on the Sunday before Easter 'for people to carry small sprays of catkins of the willow in their hands'.[23] It was also customary for people to eat figs or fig pudding for tea, and the grocers' shops used to create a display of figs in the week

---

20   My own translation of the Latin hymn quoted in CAMUS (2004), p. 341: *Laudet dominum cum Petro sancto / Burgensis ecclesia in claris / lampadibus Kyneburgha et / Kyneswitha ac Tibba / In translatorem sanctarum / reliquiarum exorta est regis et populi / tempestas naufragosa sed mox / imperante domino facta est / tranquillitas magna / Nobis quoque / bene prosperetur trinitas benedicta / per nos, o beate Kyneburgha et / Kynes-witha ac Tibba. / Gloriosa dispensation dei interfector regis et martyris Oswaldi, Rex Penda, / protullit gemellas rosas Christo de sua / spina – Christianissimas filias Christo / suscipiente de pagano parente. Gloria / patri et filio et spiritui sancto.* A literal translation would be: 'Let the church of Burgh praise the Lord, together with St Peter, and, with their bright torches, let Kyneburgha and Kyneswitha and Tibba do likewise. Against the remover of the sacred relics arose a ship-wrecking storm from king and people, but soon, at the Lord's command, was made great tranquillity. May the blessed Trinity also prosper us, o blessed Kyneburgha, Kyneswitha and Tibba. By God's glorious providence the slayer of Oswald, king and martyr, King Penda, fathered two roses for Christ from his thorn – with Christ receiving these most Christian daughters from their pagan father. Glory be to the Father and to the Son and to the Holy Spirit.'
21   CAMUS (2004), p. 341
22   Dack (1899), pp. 325–6.
23   Dack (1899), p. 326.

Figure 40
Monument
to Matthew
Wyldbore, St
John's church,
Peterborough.
Photograph by
the author.

leading up to Palm Sunday, but this custom had fallen into disuse by the end of the nineteenth century.[24]

Maundy Thursday

Otherwise known as Holy Thursday. John Clare wrote, 'On Holy thursday they go round the fields opening the [meres] or land marks w[h]ere they still keep up an ancient custom [of] scambling in the mere holes[25] for sugar plums & running races for cross skittles in which old & young often join.' He added that 'there is also a curious superstition which has forgotten the cause which it origionated ... young boys & girls the sons & daughters go on purpose to be placed on their heads in the mere'.[26]

Good Friday

On 1 April 1904, which that year was Good Friday, Dack wrote in his book of newspaper cuttings:

---

24   Dack (1911), p. 11.
25   Deacon (1983), p. 289 interpreted 'mere holes' as the holes left behind by 'meer stones' once used to mark out boundaries of property or parishes, and concludes that the rituals described by Clare were a development of 'beating the bounds' on Rogation Day.
26   Deacon (1983), p. 285.

Today I was reminded of an old custom. When some hot cross buns were brought in my friend took one and giving me the bun held it with me & asked me to repeat with him the following couplet and at the same time we were to break the bun in halves –

'Half for you and half for me,
Between us two good luck shall be.'

This is said to cement friendship between the two who break the bun.

Dack added, 'It is said that those who do not eat a hot cross bun on Good Friday is liable to suffer from fire during the ensuing year. Some people keep a piece of bread made on Good Friday as a charm against fire.'[27] This would appear to be a post-Reformation adaptation of the medieval belief that a consecrated host kept in the house would protect it from fire (these also had a cross imprinted on them), a custom strenuously discouraged by the church.[28]

April

24 *St Mark's Eve*

This night was associated with divination customs, especially in the Fens.[29] John Clare described the custom of making 'dumb cake' by unmarried young women:

> On saint Marks Eve it is still a custom about us for young maids who are sometimes joined by young men to bake the 'dumb cake' a mystical ceremony which has lost [its] origin … [the] number of the partys is never to exceed three[.] they meet in silence & make the cake & at twelve o'clock they eat it[,] still without speaking[,] for if one speaks the spell is broken[.] when they have done they walk up to bed backwards & those that are to [be] married see the likeness of their sweethearts hurrying after them as if they wanted to catch them before they get into bed[,] but the maids being apprised of this beforehand take care nearly to undress them selves before they start & are ready to slip into bed before they are caught & if nothing [is] seen the token is sure to be heard in a knocking at the doors or [a] rustling in the house as soon as they have left[;] & be convinced that it comes from nothing else but the desired cause [they] take care to turn out the cats & dogs on that night [in] particular[.]

However, the 'dumb cake' divination rite could take a more sinister turn, since 'those that are to die unwed see nor hear [no]thing but have terrible dreams which are sure to be of Graves & rings that fit no finger & if they do crumble [in] to dust as soon as on'. Clare noted that an alternative custom was to eat 'the yoke of an egg in silence & filling the shell with salt when the sweetheart is sure to make his appearance in some way or other before morning'.[30]

In 1905 Dack offered more details about the 'dumb cake' ritual, including a 'recipe':

27   MS note in the hand of Charles Dack, CUL, Lib.5.89.520–1, p. 71.
28   David Grummett (2016) *Material Eucharist,* Oxford: Oxford University Press, p. 107.
29   See Porter (1969), pp. 109–11.
30   Quoted in Deacon (1983), pp. 283–4.

Three girls are required. Two must make it, two bake it, two break it, and the third puts a piece under each of their pillows. Strict silence must be preserved. The two must go into the larder and jointly get the various ingredients. First they get a bowl each, hold it and wash and dry it together. Then each gets a spoonful of flour, a spoonful of water and a little salt. They must mix it together and roll it. Then they draw a line across the middle of the cake and each girl cuts her initials on opposite sides of the line. They both put it into the oven and bake it. The two take it out of the oven and break it across the line. The two pieces are given to the third girl, who places a piece under each pillow. The two girls then have to walk backwards to bed and get into bed backwards. One word or exclamation by either of the three breaks the charm. Should a gale arise or the wind appear to be rushing in the room during the baking or the rest of the preparation, if they look over their shoulders they will see their future husbands. In some districts the pieces of cake must be eaten in bed and not put under the pillows, but nothing must be drunk before breakfast. When making the cake they must stand on something they have never stood on before.

There are a number of differences between Clare's and Dack's versions of the 'dumb cake' ceremony; Clare suggests that both men and women can be involved, and does not assign specific roles to individuals, while Dack does not mention the idea of an apparition of a future husband pursuing a girl upstairs. However, both were clearly describing the same procedure, and it is likely that Dack obtained the additional detail in his account from a woman who had herself baked the 'dumb cake'. He also noted a variant of the ritual:

A dried salt fish eaten before going to bed in silence and getting into bed backwords (*sic.*) causes one's future husband to appear in a dream with a glass of water in his hand if a teetotaller, or a glass of beer if he is not one. One old woman over 40 years ago said she had tried it and her husband brought her a glass of beer. He was not an abstainer, but rather the reverse.[31]

The making of the 'dumb cake' was the theme of one of Clare's poems, *The Dumb Cake*, in which two girls purchase 'a fortune book' that gives them instructions on making the cake, as a result of which one of the girls (who is destined to die young) dreams of a man trying to put a ring on her finger which does not fit and falls to dust. She then has visions of open graves in the church.[32] Clare's poem essentially reproduces the same details of the ritual as he described in his 1825 letter to Hone, with the interesting addition that 'fortune books' contained instructions on how to perform the rite.

The second divination custom associated with St Mark's Eve was a vigil in the church porch to watch for the apparitions of those to be married and buried in the forthcoming year:

[T]he more stout hearted watch the church Poach (sic.)[.] they go in the evening & lay a branch of any tree [in] flower in the Poach & then return home & wait [till] 12 o

---

31 'Curious local customs: Mr. C. Dack's fascinating paper', 12 April 1905, newspaper cutting in CUL, Lib.5.89.520–1, pp. 78, 80.
32 Quoted in Deacon (1983), pp. 70–2.

Figure 41 Helpston church porch, site of the midnight vigil on St Mark's Eve. Photograph by the author.

clock at night when two goes as far as the church gate & one stays till the other fetches the bough[.] if they are to be married they will see their own persons hanging on [the] arms of their future husbands with the priest &c as if going [to] be married & as many couples of bride men & maidens as they shall see following them[,] so many months shall it be ere they are married[.] & if they are to dye unwed then the procession that [follows] them is a funeral coffin covered with a white sheet [seeming] to be born by shadows without heads[;] the number of carriers betokens the number of years [that] the partys are to live.

Clare noted that this watching ritual had regularly been observed in Helpston,

> & an odd character who had no fear calld Ben Barr a prophet usd [to] watch the poach every year & pretended to know [the] fates of every one in the villages round[,] as who shoud be married or dye in the year[,] but as few pence generally predicted a good omen he seldom prophesied the deaths of his believers.[33]

Ben Barr, who turned his willingness to watch in the church porch to pecuniary advantage, appears neither in the parish registers nor the 1762 muster roll for Helpston (which listed all adult males in the village).[34] However, Clare never stated that Barr was an inhabitant of Helpston, and his remark that Barr 'pretended to know [the] fates of every one in the villages round' would suggest that he watched in more than one church porch and may have originated from another village. A 1911 article in the *Peterborough Advertiser* reported that the custom had been practised at Paston and Thorney as well.[35]

---

33   Quoted in Deacon (1983), p. 284.
34   Deacon (1983), p. 288.
35   'A weird local custom!', *Peterborough Advertiser*, 17 May 1911, newspaper cutting in CUL, Lib.5.89.521, pp. 264–5.

In a manuscript note in his book of folklore cuttings, Dack described yet another St Mark's Eve custom that combined elements of the 'dumb cake' and porch watching rituals:

Take three tufts of grass plucked from a Churchyard[,] place them under your pillow and repeat aloud
'Let me know my fate, whether weal or woe,
Whether my rank's to be high or low,
Whether to live single or be a bride,
And the destiny my star doth provide.'
If you do this you will dream of your future.[36]

26 *Breakday*

John Clare wrote that this was the day 'when the Fen commons used to be broke as it was calld by turning in the stock'.[37]

There used to be a gathering custom – when old men & women & children used to go stone gathering in the fields[.] if one found a stone with a hole in it to put a string thro it & hang it at the masters coat button behind where if he did not discover it in a certain time they fell laughing & calling out 'riddy riddy wry rump' & claimed the boon of largess when the stone gathering was finished.[38]

30 *May Eve*

Clare recalled '(I usd to like a run at) duck under water on May eve (& thread my needle joan)[39] & tossing the cowslip balls over the garland that hung from chimney to chimney across the street'. These balls were known as 'cucking balls'.[40]

May

1 *May Day*

This was one of the major festivals of the year, whose agricultural significance was that it marked the beginning of summer pasture for the cows (although some, it seems, continued to insist on beginning this on Old May – see below):

On may day a multiplicity of sports & customs are still observed … about us [the] first cow that is turnd upon the pasture gets the Garland the last has the mankin[,] a large branch of thorn tied to her tail[.] the young men who wish to claim the favour of their

---

36   MS note in the hand of Charles Dack, CUL, Lib.5.89.520–1, p. 84.
37   John Clare, Northampton MS 15, p. 76 quoted in Deacon (1983), p. 68.
38   Quoted in Deacon (1983), p. 68.
39   According to A. E. Baker, this describes 'A game in which the players run, two and two, in rapid succession, under a handkerchief held aloft by two persons standing apart with arms aloft … under the garland which was extended from chimney to chimney across the village street.' A. E. Baker (1854) *Glossary of Northamptonshire Words and Phrases*, 2 vols, London: J. R. Smith, at vol. 1, p. 204.
40   Clare (1996–2003), vol. 5, pp. 426–7n.

favourites wait on the green till a [late] hour & then drive out the cows of the maiden [who] the[y] Love who of course wins the garland & in the ev[ening] she is considered the Queen of the May & the man wether her favourite or not claims her as his partner for the dance at night[,] a custom that she dare not refuse to comply with as she would lose her reputation & sweetheart into the bargain[,] & grow into a byeword for a shrew & be shund accordingly.[41]

Dack reported that on May Day,

> In the earlier part of the XIX Century it was the custom for a young man to get as large a branch of May in flower on 1st May and fix it to his sweethearts window. If the shutters were closed it was thrust through the diamond, and round or heart shaped openings at the top of the shutters[.] The larger the bunch and more blossoms the greater the compliment but should a quarrel have occurred and not been healed then the angry swain would fix a branch of the blackthorn in the place which should have held the may blossom.[42]

By the late nineteenth century, May Day was an important festival for children. Dack noted that the construction of May Day garlands differed north and south of the River Nene:

> The Huntingdonshire Garland is different to the Peterborough one as it is in the form of a pyramid and made up of as many bright coloured flowers as possible and the doll is placed on the top. From the bottom of the pyramid hang streamers of ribbons tissue paper & of all colours. The garland is fixed on a stick and carried by two girls[.] A Queen of the May used to be chosen from the girls who was dressed with all the finery favourable[;] she had a bunch of flowers in her hand and the garland was carried behind her by the two maids of honour. The Peterborough Garland is formed of two hoops and a stick across the middle – this is decorated with flowers & ribbons and the doll is placed inside the garland.[43]

Dack's musical skill enabled him to transcribe the words and music of the Peterborough Garland Song from the children who sang it on 1 May 1904:

> The cuckoo sings in April,
> The cuckoo sings in May,
> The cuckoo sings in June,
> In July he flies away;
> To the Greenwoods we will go,
> To the greenwoods we will go go go,
> To the Greenwoods we will go.[44]

---

41   Quoted in Deacon (1983), p. 285.
42   MS note in the hand of Charles Dack in CUL, Lib.5.89.520–1, p. 54.
43   MS note in the hand of Charles Dack in CUL, Lib.5.89.520–1, p. 86.
44   MS note in the hand of Charles Dack in CUL, Lib.5.89.520–1, p. 88. For the full text and music of the Peterborough May Garland Song see Dack (1911), pp. 11–13; details of the May Day songs also appeared in the *Peterborough Advertiser* of 6 May 1911 (newspaper cutting in CUL, Lib.5.89.520–1, pp. 223–4).

Dack provided a more extensive description of May Day festivities for the *Peterborough Advertiser* in 1911, when he noted that the customs were already becoming more homogeneous and less individual:

> The May Day Garlands are still to be seen in Peterborough and the District, but their number and varieties decrease year by year. Only a few years ago garlands were to be seen everywhere carried by two children and accompanied by four or more other children adorned with wreaths of flowers, ribbons, or coloured paper streamers, a Doll (the Queen of the May) inside the garland, which was carefully covered with a clean linen cover, and the cover only raised when the group stopped before a house or any kind-looking person who appeared to be a likely one to give a penny for the sight.

An attempt had even been made in Peterborough to organise the May Day festivities, a sign perhaps of the conscious revival (and invention) of tradition that characterised Victorian and Edwardian culture:

> Some years ago the late Mr. John Thomas House and Mr. F. Holdich, of Peterborough, endeavoured to make a festival of the day, and a large procession of garlands, headed by Mr. F. Holdich with a very large garland, paraded the streets, and a tea was given to all who formed the procession, and prizes were given for the best garland. At the Bishop's Road School a May Day Festival is held and a Crowning the Queen of the May in which the principal girls take part.[45]

Dack's comments are a valuable insight into the transformation of May Day into a festival for children and its subsequent appropriation by primary schools. This development undoubtedly helped preserve the festival, with many schools continuing to celebrate May Day into the 1980s and 1990s (and even into the twenty-first century), but it also emptied the May Day customs of some of their more disorderly elements.

12 *Old May Eve*

In spite of the shift from the Julian to the Gregorian calendar in 1752, people continued to celebrate May Eve and May Day according to the old calendar in Peterborough until the beginning of the twentieth century.[46] John Hales reported a custom at Castor on Old May Eve, when the cows were brought to graze on the common for the summer:

> The best jumpers were selected from each farm and at twelve o'clock on the Eve of Old May Day, were taken to the dyke or drain, at either the 'Plash' or the 'Brook' which ever field was to be grazed for that season, and a man had the halter, one to each cow on the

---

45   Charles Dack, 'Local May-Day customs', *Peterborough Advertiser*, 6 May 1911, newspaper cutting in CUL, Lib.5.89.520–1, p. 223.

46   According to Dack, people continued to celebrate Old May Day on 12 rather than 13 May in the twentieth century, in spite of the fact that the Julian and Gregorian calendars were by then thirteen rather than twelve days apart (Dack, 'Local May-Day customs', *Peterborough Advertiser*, 6 May 1911, newspaper cutting in CUL, Lib.5.89.520–1, p. 224).

opposite side of the dyke to the cows, another man stood with a large stick, and at the first stroke of twelve he struck and there was then quite as much excitement as there is at any of our great races, as the first cow over had the greatest prize, vis:– the 'Garland', the second the 'Poesy', and the third the 'Whistle Spoon'.

Hales also reported an Old May Eve custom that was markedly similar to the one described by Clare in Helpston on May Eve:

> [O]n the same evening it was customary to place bushes in a conspicuous place at the greater part of the farm houses. I have seen them put down the chimney, the bushy part sticking out of the top. There were three grades of bushes; the first the white thorn, for the prettiest and cleanest damsel; second, the blackthorn for the slattern; the third, for one of loose morals; the division of these favours often causes a fight between the young men of the period.[47]

It would seem that the inhabitants of Castor were even less willing to transfer their customs to the new Gregorian May Day than the villagers of Helpston, unless Hales was inaccurate in attributing all of these May customs to the old Julian date.

13 *Old May Day*

The May Day procession in Peterborough was repeated on Old May Day 'but it depends for its success on the state of the weather on May 1st'.[48] At Castor, the cows which had won the races on Old May Eve were paraded through the village on the night of Old May Day itself, 'with their honours on their horns but woe to the last; its honour was not on its horns but on its tail and was called the "Morkin or Dishclout" and was considered a disgrace for that season to the unfortunate lad who tended it'.[49]

Pentecost

Otherwise known as Whitsunday. This was the main time in the year when 'sugar cupping' was practised at East Well in Helpston (see Chapter 3).

29 *Oak Apple Day*

This custom commemorated the Restoration of King Charles II (and the English monarchy) on 29 May 1660, and oak was worn to commemorate the night the king spent in an oak tree hiding from Parliamentarian soldiers:

> Sprays of oak are worn in the button-hole, in the hat, and by some boys in the tops of their boots, just hidden by their trousers. The oak leaf and apple combined is the desired object to wear, and on the evening of May 28th you will see lads carrying arms full of oak sprays for themselves and friends. On the morning of the 29th most people used to wear their oak; but except amongst the few old inhabitants it is confined chiefly to

---

47   CAMUS (2004), p. 349.
48   Dack (1899), p. 327.
49   CAMUS (2004), p. 349.

schoolboys, and you will hear the challenge 'Show your oak,' and woe betide the lad who has not a piece to show, however small it may be, as he is subject to nips and pinches, and he must not retaliate; and then comes in the artful dodger who, looking very innocent, and not showing any signs of the oak, when challenged turns round slightly, raises his trousers showing the oak in his boot, and letting out a vigorous kick, or, in Peterborough schoolboy phrase, 'Hocks their shins'. But at midday, when the clock strikes twelve, away goes every piece of oak, no more is to be shown; as after that time the wearer is liable to be pinched for showing his oak, as before that time he was punished for not having it.[50]

The custom seems to have died out within a few years of Dack recording it, and a local newspaper reported in 1912 that 'Our old friend C[harles] D[ack] recalls for our especial edification that he "did not see a single oak apple this year".'[51]

June

Sheep shearing feast

Dack gives the following account of the traditional sheep shearing feast:

It was the custom when the shearing was finished for the Shepherds and shearers to be entertained at supper by the farmer and the farmers daughters used to make bunches of roses tied with ribbons and give one to each of the men but the head shepherd had the longest and best bunch. It was considered by the girls great fun to put a quantity of pepper in the roses so that the poor shepherds had severe fits of sneezing. Being expected the joke never failed to cause a tremendous noise of sneezing both natural and mock .... June was the month during which the feast was held. This was done as late as 1856.[52]

24 Midsummer

Although the summer solstice actually falls on 21 June it was traditionally celebrated in England on 24 June, the Feast of St John the Baptist, since this was the major Christian festival around this time. Clare recorded that 'It is a very old custom among villagers in summer time to stick a piece of greensward full of field flowers & place it as an ornament in their cottages[,] which ornaments are called Midsummer Cushions.'[53]
 Dack recorded a Midsummer divination charm for young women:

As the clock strikes Midnight take some hempseed and go into the garden and begin to throw the hempseed on the ground, repeating these words:– Hempseed I throw, / Hempseed I hoe, / He that is my true love, / Come after me and mow.

The woman was then supposed to look over her left shoulder and she would see her future husband. An alternative practice was to enter the garden backwards, maintaining

50   Dack (1899), p. 331.
51   Newspaper cutting dated 1912 in CUL, Lib.5.89.520–1, p. 213.
52   MS note in the hand of Charles Dack in CUL, Lib.5.89.520–1, p. 64.
53   John Clare, Peterborough MS A54, quoted in Deacon (1983), p. 73.

complete silence, and to pluck a rose, wrap it in paper and conceal it without looking at it until Christmas Day. The rose will still be fresh on Christmas Day, and if a woman wears it on her bosom her future husband will come and take it. [54]

29 St Peter's Day

On the patronal festival of Peterborough Minster and the city of Peterborough, the gates of the minster precincts used to be shut 'so that the Dean and Chapter may claim the exclusive "right of way"'. This day also marked the anniversary of the consecration of the new Minster in 1140.[55] After evensong, the Dean used to read from his stall a list of founders and benefactors while the congregation stood.

> And now, according to our bounden duty, let us thankfully commemorate before Almighty God our Founders and Benefactors, by whose pious liberality this our Body hath been endowed with many privileges and possessions, that, by its Ministry the Glory of God and the welfare of men may be advanced.

The Dean began with 'the labour and devotion of Peada, Wulfere and Ethelred, Kings of Mercia, by whom the first Abbey of Medeshamstead was endowed' and continued through the centuries down to Dean Marsham Argles (1814–92), 'to whose liberality we are indebted for the Bishop's throne, pulpit and marble pavement for the choir'. Most grudging was the acknowledgement of Henry VIII: 'Also we have to acknowledge the action of King Henry VIII. who, when he destroyed the monastery and plundered their possessions, spared this church, and applied a portion of the revenues of the house to found this See and Cathedral Body in the year 1541.' Dack noted that the recitation of this prayer had 'been discontinued only in the last few years', that is, between the death of Marsham Argles in 1892 and 1899, when Dack was writing.[56] The recitation of bidding prayers commemorating founders was an attempt by the post-Reformation church to honour the obligations imposed on it to pray for the souls of benefactors by countless wills and bequests – something which the established church's Protestant doctrine no longer allowed it to do.

Richard II granted a charter to the Abbot and monks for a fair to begin on St Peter's Day lasting for eight days, although by 1686 the fair had contracted to just one day.[57] By the nineteenth century it was known as Cherry Fair, and took place in July.

July

Cherry Fair

At this fair, held at the beginning of July, 'it was the privilege of any inhabitant to start a bough house'. The last one built was 'at the corner of Combergate ... being kept by a man named Hall, a razor-grinder, about 1835'. A peculiar privilege associated with

54   Dack (1911), pp. 14–15.
55   Gunton (1686), p. 277.
56   Dack (1899), pp. 332–3.
57   Gunton (1686), p. 26.

Figure 42 Postcard depicting the Cherry Fair in 1886

this fair, which seems to have lent it its name, was the fact that any householder could place a cherry branch over the door and sell beverages between noon and midnight to the public once the fair had been proclaimed. Dack remembered that 'about twenty years ago' (circa 1879) 'two men in Broad Street ... cleared their shops and sold tea, coffee and refreshments, and announced their intention of re-starting the old bough houses: but the authorities stepped in'.[58] This was unsurprising, since the 1873 Fairs Act had led to the abolition of most traditional fairs.

24 *Feast of St Wulfade and St Rufinus*

Before the Reformation, this was the day on which the monks commemorated the two legendary sons of King Wulfhere of Mercia whom the king supposedly killed in a rage for converting to Christianity. The heart of St Wulfade was supposed to have been concealed in the well in the Minster cloister by St Chad (see Chapter 1).

August

5 *St Oswald's Day*

Before the Reformation the incorrupt arm of St Oswald was carried in procession in Peterborough Minster on this day.[59] After the Reformation a fair continued to be held on this day, but it seems to have fallen into abeyance during the Interregnum (1649–60). Gunton noted:

---

58   Dack (1899), p. 341.
59   Higham (1988), p. 18.

The Town of Peterburgh hath in our memory kept another Fair upon the Feast of S. Oswald, August 5. but I have not yet met with the Original of it: which Fair is now quite fallen, and like to be buried in obscurity, unless some well-willers to the Priviledge shall endeavour to restore it according to its ancient custom, if the time of Harvest will permit.[60]

September

Harvest Home

Taking place towards the end of August or beginning of September, Harvest Home was one of the great festivals of the English year whose possible pagan origins are discussed in Chapter 1 above. Dack recorded in 1905:

> The Harvest Home suppers are now almost a thing of the past. I went to one about eight years ago [c. 1897], and suppose it will be the last. It is held when the last load of corn is taken home. This load used to be decorated with boughs and flowers, and the youngest boys employed used to ride on it, singing: 'Harvest Home, Harvest Home, / Two plum puddings are better than one; / We've ploughed, we've sowed, / We've reaped, we've mowed, / We've got our Harvest Home.' In the evening the supper was held, and afterwards songs sung. The eldest labourer used to propose the health of the Master and the Mistress, and a Harvest Home song would be sung.[61]

The labourers would also cry 'Largess!', a reminder of an old tradition that the master was bound to give gifts of money to the labourers at Harvest Home, although Dack observed that by his time the cry was 'merely an old custom' and rarely resulted in the labourers receiving money. Harvest Home was also known as 'Wheat Hovel Day'. Dack recorded several of the songs sung at the Harvest Home but lamented, 'I wish I could remember the old songs which are now forgotten.'[62]

Clare noted that traditional games were often played at the end of the harvest supper, such as 'Booted Hogs', which was a punishment for 'such boys who have carelessly neglected their duty in the harvest … as letting their cattle get finded or overthrowing their leads &c':

> A long form is placed in the Kitchen upon which the boys who have worked well sit as a tenor & disgrace to the rest in a bent position with their hands laid on each others backs & forming a bridge for the hogs (as the truant boys are calld) to pass over while a strong chap stands on each side with a boot legging soundly strapping them as they scuffle over the bridge which is done as fast as there ingenuity can carry them.[63]

60   Gunton (1686), p. 166.

61   'Curious local customs: Mr. C. Dack's fascinating paper', 12 April 1905, newspaper cutting in CUL, Lib.5.89.520–1, p. 82.

62   Dack (1911), p. 16.

63   Quoted in Deacon (1983), p. 291. For other traditional games not assigned to a specific time of the year see pp. 290–2 and Eric Robinson (2013) 'John Clare: games, pastimes, sports and customs', *Wordsworth*

14 *Holy Rood Day*

John Clare wrote that:

> On Holy rood day it is faithfully & confidently believed both by old & young that the Devil goes a nutting on that day & I have heard a many people thought it a tale till they venturd to the woods [on] that day when they smelt such a strong smell of brimstone as nearly stifled them before they coud escape out again ... & the [*illegible*] to his great disappointment finds that the devil will [not] even let his black berrys alone & he believes them after that day to be poisend by his touch.[64]

15 *St Kyneburgha's Day*

Before the removal of St Kyneburgha to Peterborough in the eleventh century her feast day was celebrated on the anniversary of her death, 15 September. According to the eighteenth-century antiquary William Stukeley, on this day a phantom coach and horses was supposed to carry 'Lady Ketilborough' (a corruption of Kyneburgha) along Ermine Street (see Chapter 3).

20 *Vigil of St Matthew's Day*

According to the original charter of 1439 for Bridge Fair it was supposed to be proclaimed on the Vigil of St Matthew's Day, but by the nineteenth century the fair had migrated to the first week of October.

29 *Michaelmas*

The Feast of St Michael and All Angels was a lucky one for washing: 'If a woman has a fine day for washing the first time after Michaelmas day she will have fine washing days all through the year.'[65]

30 *Feast of Saints Tancred, Torthred and Tova*

In the Middle Ages the feast of the hermit saints of Thorney killed by the Danes was celebrated on this day at Thorney Abbey and in the Deepings.

October

1st Tuesday, Wednesday and Thursday, Bridge Fair

Originally supposed to start on the Vigil of St Matthew's Day (21 September), by the nineteenth century Bridge Fair had migrated to the beginning of October and was always proclaimed on the Tuesday before continuing for two more days. The Abbots of Peterborough had the right to hold a fair on both sides of the River Nene beginning on the vigil of the Feast of St Matthew (20 September) and lasting for three days, according to a charter of Henry VI of 14 July 1439:

Circle, 44, pp. 56–60.

64 Quoted in Deacon (1983), p. 285.

65 MS note in the hand of Charles Dack in CUL, Lib.5.89.520–1, p. 199.

Let them have forever a fair in individual years on the bridge of Peterborough next to the River Nene, as much in the County of Northampton as in the County of Huntingdon, on each side of the bridge in the dominion of the said same Abbot and Convent, to last for three days, that is to say, holding it on the vigil and on the day of St Matthew the Apostle and on the next day after the same feast: unless that fair should be to the detriment of neighbouring fairs.[66]

The Bridge Fair was unusual in crossing the boundary between two counties, but this can be explained by the fact that the Abbey owned land on both sides of the Nene; since the grant was to the Abbey (and not to the city), the Abbot was within his rights to hold the fair on both sides of the river. However, the dissolution of the Abbey in 1539 threw the continuation of the fair into doubt, since the Abbey to whom the grant had been made no longer existed. Henry VIII had to re-grant the privilege of holding Bridge Fair to the Dean and Chapter of Peterborough Cathedral.[67]

Prior to 1874, at a quarter to noon the High Bailiff of the city, as the representative of the Dean and Chapter, accompanied by the Magistrates, Feoffees, Improvement Commissioners, lay clerks, halberd bearers and town crier left the Minster precincts. The beadle read the proclamation of Bridge Fair three times: in the marketplace, in the middle of the bridge between Peterborough and Huntingdonshire, and in the meadow where the fair was held.[68] In 1874 the city was incorporated, meaning that local government passed out of the hands of the Dean and Chapter to a corporation, and thereafter the procession consisted of the Mayor and Corporation and left from the Guildhall. The town crier would proclaim the fair:

OYES. OYES. OYES. This is to give Notice that the Fair Called Bridge Fair will be held and kept to-day, to-morrow and the next day, as well in the County of Huntingdonshire as in Northamptonshire, by the order of Her Majesty's Secretary of State, dated May 13th, 1878, and made in pursuance of the Fairs Act, 1878. Therefore all Persons are required to behave themselves Soberly and Civilly and to pay their respective dues and demands according to the law of the Realm and the rights of the Corporation of the City and Borough of Peterborough the owners of the aforesaid Fair. God Save the Queen.[69]

In the days when the lay clerks joined the procession with the High Bailiff, they used to sing 'Amen' after the proclamation was read, although it is unclear whether or not this original proclamation was the Latin text of Henry VI's or Henry VIII's charter.

---

66 Gunton (1686) pp. 165–6: … *in perpetuum habeant unam Feriam singulis annis apud pontem de Peter-burgh juxta aquam de Neene, tam in Comitatu Northt. quam in Com. Hunt. ex utraque parte ejusdem pontis in dominio eorundem Abbatis, & Conventus ibidem per tres dies duraturam, viz. in vigilia, & in die Sancti Matthaei Apostoli, & in Crastino ejusdem festi tenens: Nisi Feria illa sit ad nocumentum vicinarum Feriarum.*

67 I have not been able to locate the text of Henry VIII's charter, but it would have followed a standard form and resembled the earlier grant.

68 Dack (1911), p. 14 noted, 'A copy of the proclamation was fortunately obtained for me before the old Beadle died. He had not a copy but used to repeat it from memory.' Unfortunately Dack did not include the text of the pre-1878 proclamation.

69 Dack (1899), p. 334.

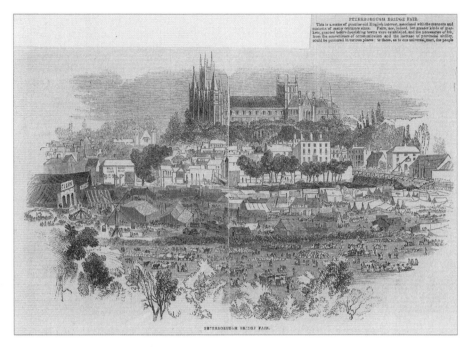

Figure 43 The Bridge Fair in 1844, engraving from the *Illustrated London News*

After the proclamation, the Mayor and Corporation adjourned to the booth belonging to the Cross Keys inn, the oldest public house in the city, where they dined on champagne and sausages. Indeed, pork, bacon, pies and sausages were central to Bridge Fair, and small pigs were bred specially for the occasion known as 'Bridge Fairers'. For 2s 6d a day any public house could obtain a licence to set up a booth and sell alcohol at the fair, and it was customary for tradesmen to entertain their loyal customers, who would bring along numerous friends to enjoy the hospitality. At one time the waggons bringing people to the fair from all over the Soke of Peterborough were decorated with evergreens and tree branches.[70]

In 1905 the Mayor and Corporation voted to discontinue the public proclamation and proclamation procession because members of the public had laughed at and made fun of them. The vote occasioned an outcry in the pages of the *Peterborough Advertiser*, with numerous correspondents (including Charles Dack) criticising the Mayor and Corporation for their decision.[71] The fair itself continued, but notice was given by a handbill fixed to the town hall and the traditional sausage supper was discontinued. The Bridge Fair itself was discontinued in 1914 owing to war-time austerity but was revived in 1929, when the proclamation ceremony was also reinstated (although this time the Mayor himself, rather than a town crier, read the 1878 version of the proclamation).

---

70 Dack (1899), p. 335.
71 Newspaper cuttings of 6, 12, 14 October, 30 November 1905 in CUL, Lib.5.89.520–1 pp. 102–13.

The proclamation ceremony was abolished again in 1974 but revived again in 1976,[72] and the fair continues in spite of the fact that the fair meadow has long since been built over. The sausage supper has also been revived, although it is now a charity event held in Peterborough's new town hall rather than at the fair itself.[73] Bridge Fair remains one of only a handful of medieval English fairs that has existed continuously (apart from the short disruption of 1914–29) down to the present day, and is one of Peterborough's most cherished traditions.

November

11 *Martinmas*

Originally the Feast of St Martin of Tours. Dack observed that 'old people still watch for the direction of the wind at noon on this day as they believe it will continue in that quarter for the next three months'.[74]

22 *St Cecilia's Day*

On the feast day of the patron saint of music and musicians the Dean and Chapter used to invite the Cathedral's musical staff, the organist and the lay clerks, to a supper of boiled leg of mutton at a local hotel. The lay clerks entertained the company by singing.[75]

23 *St Clement's Day*

Blacksmiths, brewers and carpenters used to celebrate their patron saint with suppers on this day, but the practice had died out by the late nineteenth century.[76]

25 *Queen Katern's Day*

St Catherine's Day (25 November) was known in the city as 'Queen Katern's day'. Women and girls from the workhouse would dress in white, holding distaffs in their hands, while one woman wore a paper crown on her head. She was accompanied by a man representing the king. The women sang, 'Here comes Queen Katern, as fine as any Queen, / In a coach and six horses a-coming to be seen', with the chorus repeated between each verse, 'Some say she's alive, and some say she's dead, / But now she does appear with a crown on her head, / And a-spinning we will go.'[77] Since St Catherine of Alexandria was not a queen, it is possible that this custom reflected a dim memory of Katharine of Aragon, who was conflated with the saint (the register of St John's church for the burial of the queen on 26 June 1536 called her 'my lady Katern').[78]

---

72   'Fair brings joy to David', *Peterborough Telegraph*, online edition, 6 October 2003, peterboroughtoday. co.uk/news/environment/leisure-fair-brings-joy-to-david-1-144490, accessed 26 December 2016.

73   'Bridge fair and sausage supper invite for residents', Peterborough City Council, 15 September 2016, peterborough.gov.uk/news/council/bridge-fair-and-sausage-supper-invite-for-residents, accessed 26 December 2016.

74   Dack (1911), p. 17.

75   Dack (1899), p. 335.

76   Dack (1899), p. 335.

77   Dack (1899), p. 336.

78   Dixon (1980), p. 21.

The custom was first recorded in 1854 by Anne Elizabeth Baker who noted that, at that time, it was peculiar to Peterborough, and claimed that references to 'wheels and reels for the children of the workhouse' in the accounts of the Dean and Chapter pointed to the 'great antiquity' of the procession.[79] Peterborough was a particularly important centre for the carding and spinning of wool.[80] Dack observed that the Peterborough 'Catherine Procession' took place whatever the weather. The custom was eventually stopped in the early twentieth century by substituting it with a special dinner for the women and girls from the workhouse on 25 November.[81]

The words 'Some say she's alive, and some say she's dead' might refer to Katharine of Aragon's relegation to obscurity in Kimbolton Castle by Henry VIII, and Dack noted elsewhere that Peterborough lacemakers, who likewise celebrated St Catherine's Day as a holiday, were 'aware that Katharine of Arragon is the patron saint of the lacers' craft'.[82] On the other hand, the words 'a-spinning we will go' are clearly a reference to St Catherine as the patron saint of spinning (the major occupation of women in the workhouse), since St Catherine was martyred on a wheel.[83]

30 *Tander Day*

A corruption of St Andrew's Day. The significance of this day in Peterborough may have derived from the fact that the Minster is dedicated to St Peter, St Paul and St Andrew. The day was celebrated by the city's lacemakers by men and women both cross-dressing and drinking hot elder wine in each other's houses.[84] The day was also special for schoolboys:

> It was a curious custom called 'Tander' on St. Andrew's Day at Easton-on-the-Hill, near Peterborough, and other places, for the boys to lock the village schoolmaster out of the school and demand the rest of the day for a holiday before the door was re-opened. If the master could obtain an entrance to the school before giving his consent, the holiday was not given.[85]

December

1 *Mummers' plays*

At the beginning of December performances of mummers' plays began in Peterborough and its surrounding villages, lasting until Christmas. In the Peterborough

---

79   Baker (1854), vol. 2, pp. 436–7. However, these may simply have been payments for spinning wheels for workhouse children and do not prove that a procession then existed.

80   See Morton (1712), p. 24: 'The poorer Sort are usually employ'd in the Carding, Spinning, or Knitting of Wooll, and many others in the Combing and Weaving it; So much the Woollen Manufactures have of late taken Place in this City'.

81   Charles Dack, 'A forgotten festival', *The Golden Penny*, 28 November 1903, p. 431.

82   Charles Dack, 'The Feast of St Katherine', undated newspaper cutting in CUL, Lib.5.89.520–1, p. 97.

83   A report in the *Peterborough Advertiser* of 12 March 1902 that the Catherine procession used to take place on May Day in Stanground is surely mistaken.

84   Dack (1911), p. 18.

85   'Curious local customs: Mr. C. Dack's fascinating paper', 12 April 1905, newspaper cutting in CUL, Lib.5.89.520–1, p. 82.

area the play was called a 'Morris Dance' and its performers 'Morris Dancers' or 'Morry Dancers', a title that may have derived from the fact that the same men who performed the play danced Morris at other times of the year.[86] It is unclear how old this tradition is. In 1620 the Peterborough feoffees received 3s 4d from 'players for breakinge downe ye stayres of ye towne Hall',[87] and received 12d in October 1628 from 'Mr. Joanes the player, for sheweinge of his puppites, and for sheweinge tricks in our common hall'.[88]

Apart from these early mentions of what may have been mummers, John Clare's description and partial transcription of the 'Morris Dance' as performed at Helpston is one of the earliest detailed accounts of an English mummers' play.[89] The text of the Peterborough play, which was also performed as far afield as Milton Hall, was published in the *Peterborough Advertiser* in 1902, based on the recollections of a man who performed it in 1847 and 1848;[90] a partial text of the Yaxley play was also published in the newspaper in that year.[91] Dack seems to have had access to a slightly different variant of the play,[92] as may Thomas Ratcliffe, who alluded to the mummers' plays in an article on Christmas traditions in the *Peterborough Advertiser* in 1908.[93] All of these sources are included as an appendix to this book.

The mummers' play usually featured just four characters: the King of Egypt, Prince (or King) George, Beelzebub or the Buffoon, and the Doctor. The basic plot of the play features an argument between the King of Egypt and Prince George in which either George or Beelzebub is apparently killed, at which point the Doctor restores the slain character to life. Clare observed of the Helpston play that 'it appears to have been a burlesque parody on some popular story at the time but it has been so mutilated by its different performers that I coud not make sense of it tho I tried to transcribe from the mouths [of] 3 or 4 persons who had all been actors in it'.[94] Clare was astute in trying to transcribe the play from more than one actor rather than relying on one source; the play was entirely learned orally by its performers and never written down, and it is clear that even the play performed in one village would vary in details from one performance to the next. Clare complained that the play was 'destitute [of] common sense' but a fragment of his transcription does survive. Deacon thought that the remainder of Clare's transcription must survive somewhere, but it is also possible that Clare gave up trying to write the play down and instead simply summarised the action.

---

86   See Deacon (1983), p. 69.
87   W. T. Mellows (ed.) (1937) *Peterborough Local Administration: Minutes and Accounts of the Feoffees and Governors of the City Lands*, Northamptonshire Records Society 10. Kettering: Northamptonshire Record Society, p. 30.
88   Mellows (1937), p. 48.
89   Deacon (1983), pp. 285–6 (description), 293 (partial transcription).
90   'The Peterborough Mummers' Play as played at Milton: a folk-drama of fifty years ago', *Peterborough Advertiser*, 23 April 1902.
91   'The Mummers Play at Yaxley', *Peterborough Advertiser*, 12 March 1902.
92   See Dack (1899), pp. 336–7.
93   Thomas Ratcliffe, 'Some Yule and New Year old customs', *Peterborough Advertiser,* 28 December 1908.
94   Quoted in Deacon (1983), p. 285.

The apparent lack of sense in the play seems to have derived from its place in the oral tradition, in which faithful transmission of the material mattered more than ensuring the drama made sense to its audience. The play was a ritual performance, expected every Christmas, in which coherence and comprehensibility were less important than familiarity and tradition. There are some recognisable similarities between the mummers' plays and the Punch and Judy puppet shows that gradually supplanted them in the late nineteenth century; the character of the Doctor was borrowed by Punch and Judy shows from the mummers' plays, and the devil ('Beelzebub') features in both. However, the Peterborough mummers' play references Punch and Judy directly when Beelzebub (equivalent to the Buffoon in the Helpston play) describes himself as 'Punchinello'. This is unusual both because mummers rarely referenced Punch and Judy but also because Punch was rarely called by his old Italian name Punchinello by the mid-nineteenth century.[95]

Clare noted that the 'Buffoon' of the Helpston play had 'a hunch back & a bell between [his] legs … & he generally carries in his hand a hugh club'. The grotesque hunchback, bells and stick are recognisable characteristics of Punchinello. In *The Shepherds Calendar*, Clare describes the mummers' play and apparently identifies the Buffoon as harlequin ('And harlequin a laugh to raise / Wears his hump back and tinkling bell'), but it seems more likely that the assignment of this name to the character is just poetic licence on Clare's part.[96] The same character in the Yaxley play was called 'Old Grubb'. E. K. Chambers concluded in the 1930s that the Beelzebub of the mummers' play was derived ultimately from the devil of the medieval mystery plays, and that the club and pan he carries are meant to punish sinners. Chambers rejected speculation that the Beelzebub figure was a decayed representation of an ancient club-wielding deity.[97] The gradual transformation of the devil from a terrifying figure into an amusing caricature was a feature of English popular culture between the sixteenth and nineteenth centuries.[98]

George Thompson, the former mummer who gave the text of the Peterborough play to the *Peterborough Advertiser* in 1902, had Beelzebub appear to fall down dead, whereas in 1899 Dack stated that either the King or 'St George' was slain. This is a significant difference between the two accounts, and since Dack's description is sketchier it may be that he was in error. Alternatively, it is possible that the mummers varied the elements of the story from year to year or from place to place.[99] Christmas was traditionally a time of misrule and inversion of customs,[100] and an inversion of the customary plot could have embodied the topsy-turvy nature of the season. The Doctor, who according to Dack's version of the Peterborough play claims to be an exorcist, resembles the popular English folk-saint Dr John Schorne, who was supposed to have confined the devil in a boot. In

95 I am indebted to Virginie Ganivet for this information.
96 Deacon (1983), p. 69.
97 E. K. Chambers (1933) *The English Folk-Play*, Oxford: Clarendon, p. 167.
98 See Darren Oldridge (2010) *The Devil in Tudor and Stuart England*, 2nd edn, Stroud: History Press, pp. 35–7.
99 Indeed, Mr Barnes, the elderly Yaxley man who described the Yaxley play to the *Peterborough Advertiser* in March 1902, confirmed that this was the case.
100 See Hutton (1996), pp. 95–111.

Figure 44 Peterborough-based Pig Dyke Molly, pictured here in Peterborough city centre in September 2015, provide a contemporary take on English traditional dance. Reproduced with the kind permission of photographer Chris Porsz.

1911 Dack claimed that the Doctor made his entrance on another actor playing a horse – something not included in the 1902 script, which again suggests that Dack had access to an alternative version.[101]

In 1968 Mike Herring, a member of Peterborough Folk Club, revived a version of the Peterborough mummers' play, which was performed in November and December 1968 and 1969. Although revivals drawing partly on the Peterborough play have since taken place in Whittlesey there has been no subsequent revival in Peterborough.[102] No revival seems to have exactly reproduced or incorporated all of the details of the Peterborough play that can be gleaned from local newspapers.

In addition to the mummers' play, Clare described another folk play which is not assigned to any specific time of the year, 'the dusty or deaf miller':

> The dusty or deaf miller appears in the room with a hunch back & a brush in one hand & a basket in the other[.] his man a kind of Tom fool accompanys him with a pair of bellows & a smelling bottle[.] the millers face is whitened with choak [i.e. chalk] or whitening[.] in his basket he has bread & cheese & a bottle of ale which he places on a table behind

101   Dack (1911), p. 18.

102   See an unpublished article by Maureen James, 'The Peterborough Folk Club Mummers Play – an interesting history!', Mummers Unconvention, Bath, 16 November 2012.

him were his wife is placed as seemingly unknown to him who takes it away as fast as he places it thereon[.] he affects to be surprised & pretending deafness runs oer a mess of sensless gibberish to his man whom he beats for the suppos'd theft till at last knocking his brush behind him [he] accidentally brings his wife to the ground which coming to his knowledge throws him into a great consternation & instantly begins to have recourse to a remedy for bringing her to life which is done by using the bellows … & the smelling bottle[.] on her recovery they hobble out of the room & the farce concludes.[103]

The tradition of folk dance and folk drama lives on in Peterborough through the revivals of groups such as Peterborough-based Pig Dyke Molly, whose performances are a contemporary take on local traditions of 'plough witches'.

11 *Old St Andrew's Day*

Thomas Sternberg noted in the 1850s that in many places in Northamptonshire the festivities associated with St Andrew's Day (including cross-dressing for men and women and drinking hot elder wine) were observed not on 30 November but according to the old Julian calendar.[104] This may well have been the case at Peterborough, although it is not mentioned by Dack.

13 *St Tibba's Day*

Before the translation of her body to Peterborough Abbey in the eleventh century, the feast day of St Tibba, sister of St Kyneburgha and Abbess of Ryhall, was celebrated at Castor on this day.[105]

14 *Bishop White's Charity*

On this day 10 shillings were given to twenty men and women over the age of 60 who were able to correctly recite the Lord's Prayer, the Ten Commandments and the Apostles' Creed without a mistake, following the prescriptions of the will of Bishop Thomas White (1628–98). Dack noted that the inhabitants of the almshouses were often coached by charitable visitors.[106] In 1911 the *Peterborough Advertiser* described a conversation between some of the old women about their visitors:

> Many years ago on the occasion of distributing White's Charity on the 14th December, a number of old ladies who were competing for the 10s. were discussing the many good qualities of their pastors' wives and district visitors. Each one went one better than her predecessor in expiating [sic. for 'expatiating'] on the charity, kindness, visits, and every possible virtue it was possible to name. One old lady, however, kept silent, and looked on the others with a stoney stare and an air of great superiority. Her silence at last attracted the notice of the others, and they turned to her and said, 'And where do you attend Mrs, — ?' 'Me? Where do I attend? Why, I go to the Minster and have been

---

103 Quoted in Deacon (1983), p. 291.
104 See Roud (2006), p. 363.
105 Story (1883), p. 34.
106 Dack (1899), p. 336.

there for forty years; and thank goodness there's no one there to worrit you about your trumpery soul.'[107]

20 *St Thomas' Eve*

Clare wrote that 'on St Tomases Eve it is a common custom for the young girls to lay a red peeld onion under their pillows to dream of their sweethearts'.[108]

21 *St Thomas' Day*

Known elsewhere in the country as 'Thomasing', on this day it was the custom for old people to go from house to house asking for money, since St Thomas was the patron saint of the elderly. In 1827 Earl Fitzwilliam 'distributed bread to 1,800 poor persons' on St Thomas' Day.[109] In the Peterborough area old women went 'a-gooding'. This meant that the women collected copper coins or threepences from homes and tradesmen, before having a tea party from the proceeds.[110] Elsewhere Dack described the practice as 'gurding' and associated it specifically with the widows of Farcet, noting that 'the amount collected in this village was sufficient for the women to have 2 [shillings] each'.[111] In 1911 Dack observed that the custom was 'fast passing away'.[112]

24 *Christmas Eve*

In the late nineteenth century, Christmas Eve featured large and elaborate displays of meat in butchers' shops:

> The shops are gaily trimmed with evergreens, paper flowers, gas-jets, etc. and to one inside the shop the display of the meats and the provisions is a sight worth seeing, while the streets are thronged with people criticising the shows. Last Christmas [1898] there were prizes – silver cups – for the best display. Drapers and other shops are all, of course, dressed out too, but this is essentially the butchers' show.[113]

28 *Holy Innocents Day*

Traditionally known in England as Childermas, in Peterborough this day was called 'Dyzemass Day' and it was considered a day on which it was unlucky to begin anything. Dack noted that 'about sixty or seventy years ago [i.e. in the 1840s] many old people kept this day more sacred than an ordinary Sunday',[114] presumably meaning that they observed the day as a Sabbath and abstained from any work or recreation.

---

107 'Bishop White's Charity', *Peterborough Advertiser*, 9 November 1911, newspaper cutting in CUL, Lib.5.89.520–1, p. 96.
108 Quoted in Deacon (1983), p. 286.
109 Jones (2014), p. 358.
110 Dack (1899), p. 336.
111 MS note in the hand of Charles Dack in CUL, Lib.5.89.520–1, p. 82.
112 Dack (1911), p. 18.
113 Dack (1911), p. 340. For an account of this 'meat show' in 1866 see Jones (2014), p. 366.
114 Dack (1911), p. 19.

Appendix

The Peterborough mummers' plays

John Clare's description of the Helpston mummers' play, 1825[1]

The Morris Dance is very popular now with us they begin to go round the week before Christmas[.] it appears to have been a burlesque parody on some popular story at the time but it has been so mutilated by its different performers that I coud not make sense of it tho I tried to transcribe from the mouths [of] 3 or 4 persons who had all been actors in it[.] these are [the] characters[:] 2 of them the Kean & Young of the piece[2] [are] finely dressed their hats are deckorated with carpenters shavings & cut paper & without side their cloaths they wear [a] white shirt hung with ribbons of different colors a silk hankerchief serves them for a sash & another slung over their shoulders is a belt for their swords which are some-times real & sometimes wooden ones[.] the third character is a sort of Buffoon grotesquely dressed with a hunch back & a bell between [his] legs together with a tail trailing behind [him] his face is [is] blacked & he generally carries in his hand a hugh club[.] [The] 4th is a docter dressd as much in character as their taste or circumstances allows[.] the plot of the thing is some thing as follows[.] The Kean of the Drama steps in first & on [making] a sort of prologue describes himself to be a no less personage than the king of Egypt[.] his errand appears to be to demand his lost son who seems to have married a lady not worthy [of the] heir of Egypt or to be confind in prison[,] for it is so destitute [of] common sense that you can not tell which[;] & if as they refuse [his] enquireys his champion prince George is calld on who after talking a great deal of his wonderfull feats in slaying dragons & kicking his enemys as small as flyes begins [a] dialogue with his majesty[.] then the fool is introduced with his bell who gives a humerous description of himself [&] his abilitys when all three joins in the dialogue & instantly [a] quarrel is created between the Kean & Young from what [cause] I know not & they draw their swords & fight[.] the fool [gets] between them to part them & pretending [*illegible*] to be wounded falls down as dead when the other confesses that the wounded [clown] is the kings own son in disguise whose rage is instantly turnd to sorrow & the doctor is calld in & a large reward is offered him if he can restore him to life[;] who after enumerating [his] vast powers in medical skill & knowledge declares the [person] to be only in a trance & on the doctors touching him he rises & they all join hands & end the Drama with a dance & song.

1   Quoted in Deacon (1983), pp. 285–6.
2   Deacon (1983), p. 289 suggests that these names were adopted by the mummers after two notable actors of the day, Edmund Kean and Charles Mayne Young.

Fragment of the Helpston mummers' play transcribed by John Clare from 'J[ohn] Billings an old actor in it'[3]

Prologue: Here comes I that never came before
  With three merry actors standing at the door
  They can both dance & likewise sing
  & if you please they shall step in
  Gentlemen & or ladys all Im glad to see you here
  Im come to let you know it wont be long before my actors doth appear
  Tho my company is but small
  All do the best we can to please you all
  To get your love & gain your favour
  Well do the best of our endeavour
  Now at this time Ive done my doom
  I must turn back with speed & give my actors room.

King of Egypt: Room room brave guards make room
  & let the king of Egypt in
  I am the king of Egypt as plainly doth appear
  Im come to seek my son my son is only here
  & if you dont consent to what I say
  Step in prince George & clear the way

Prince George: Here comes I prince George a champion bold
  & with my bloody spear I won three crowns of gold
  I fit the firey dragon & brought him to a slaughter
  & by that means I won the king of Egypts daughter
  I kickt him & I smackt him as small as any flies
  & I sent him to Jamaica to make much pies

  Here comes I with my swish swash & swagger
  With my cockt hat & glittering dagger
  Ive come to court a damsel.

Charles Dack's description of the Peterborough mummers' play, 1899[4]

Before Christmas, the Waits come round, and also the Morrice Dancers. These last are in the adjacent villages, and the old play is gone through. There is Belzebub, who comes in first, and says:–

  Here I come, Great Belzebub,
  Under my arm I carry my club;
  In my hand a dripping pan,
  Don't you think I'm a jolly old man?

---

3   Peterborough MS B3, p. 57 (quoted in Deacon (1983), p. 293.
4   From Dack (1899), pp. 336–7.

There is the fight between King, or St. George, and Belzebub, in which King, or St. George, is apparently killed, and the Doctor comes in and says:–

Doctor:	"I'm the Doctor!"
Belzebub:	"What can you do?"
Doctor:	"I can cure pains within and pains without,
	Love-sick palsy and the Gout;
	And if the Devil's in I cast him out."

Several other characters take part; St. George becomes alive again, and they finish up by a general dance.

Another group goes round the farmhouses as King Cole and his party. He enters, and says:–

Old King Cole was a jolly old soul,
A jolly old soul was he;
He calls for his glass,
(A servant here comes in with jug of ale and glasses.)
He calls for his pipe,
(A lad brings in some clay pipes and tobacco.)
And he calls for his fiddlers three.

Then come in the musicians with the party and begin to play merry jigs, and the party dance is a grotesque manner. They are also called the mummers.

'The Mummers Play at Yaxley'[5]

Yaxley Mummers, or Morris Dancers, or Morry Dancers as Mr. Barnes called them, were sixty or seventy years ago a great local institution. They performed an unwritten play, which resembles in many respects the plays of mummers in other parts of England. Mr. Barnes, as a youth, formed one of these mummers, and still remembers some parts of the play, which used to be performed in the principal houses of the village about three weeks before Christmas. The players were dressed in various and fantastic styles, with an abundance of coloured ribbons, to represent different characters. Besides the actors there was always one fiddler with them, and the prelude to the play was said at the door of the house visited as follows:

Here comes I as never come before,
Three merry actors at the door,
We can both fiddle, dance, and sing,
And by your leave we will step in.

The Morris Dancers having been invited in the play began. One of the characters was King George, who announced himself as:

Here comes I, King George, the champion bold,
Who by my bloody spear has won three crowns of gold.

Another was the bad man of the piece:

---

5   From the *Peterborough Advertiser*, 12 March 1902.

Here comes I, Old Lord Grubb,
Under my shoulder I carry my club,
Under my chin a dripping pan,
Don't you think me a handsome old man.

He used his club to such purpose that one of the actors was soon sprawling on his back, and the cry is raised:

Ten pounds for a doctor a dead man to cure.

This brings the doctor, who is wonderfully clever. "Oh, he could cure a lot of things" laughed Mrs. Barnes, at the recollection of the play. But the finale had to be altered according to circumstances, for some of the houses visited objected to dancing. In that case the play finished up with:

He is not dead, but lays along,
We'll raise him up and have a song.

Whereupon the fiddler fiddled, and the Morris Dancers and the maids of the house all joined in a series of round dances amid boisterous mirth, a big room or kitchen in the farmhouses being cleared for the purpose.

'The Peterborough mummers' play as played at Milton: a folk-drama of fifty years ago'[6]

We are indebted to Mr. George Thompson, of Westgate, Peterborough, for particulars of the old Mummers' play at Peterborough, as it used to be rendered in the first half of the last century. Mr. George Thompson spoke it from memory – for there appears to be no manuscript copy of it – to one of our representatives. He himself played it in the years 1847 and 1848, taking the character of Beelzebub on each occasion. It may be remembered that Mr. Barnes, the aged resident of Yaxley, referred in his reminiscences of that village recently published in these columns to the Mummers Play, at Yaxley, which resembled the Peterborough play, but apparently had numerous distinct variations. Like Mr. Thompson, Mr. Barnes had himself taken part in the Yaxley play. Fortunately Mr. Thompson has a retentive memory, and although it is now nearly fifty years since he took part in the play, he is able to remember the whole dialogue. Many others in the district can remember portions. Mr. Eatherley, of Woodstone, remembers very much of the old Mummers' Play as it was performed at Peakirk, and this again shows distinct variations from both the Peterboro' and the Yaxley plays, but it is probable that Mr. George Thompson, of Peterborough, stands alone in being able to recall to mind the entire dialogue.

At Peterborough the play was rendered at all the principal private houses and inns in the City. There were nightly performances throughout the month of December. The Mummers, or Morris Dancers, as they were called, used to be well received at Milton and also at Squire Cook's house. Mr. Thompson has still many pleasant recollections of the hearty and cordial reception the Mummers received from Earl Fitzwilliam at Milton,

---

6   From the *Peterborough Advertiser*, 23 April 1902, newspaper cutting in CUL, Lib.5.89.521, p. 299.

and also especially at the house of Mr. Wm Cook, of Peterborough, son of the late Squire Cook.

Mr. Thompson said he was taught the play orally, no portions of it that he knows were ever written. Others before him had learned it in a similar way, and it had in that manner been handed down from generation to generation.

Antiquarians and philologists have spent much time in discussing the origin of these Mummers plays. It is no part of a newspaper to discuss such scientific questions, but it is of general interest to look back upon the entertainments of our forefathers as they existed in our midst. But should anyone care to analyse this matter further there are words and phrases used in the dialogue as remembered by Mr. Thompson which may serve as a guide to the origin of the folk dramas. For instance, the King George who fought the fiery dragon and married the King of Egypt's daughter, is surely a corruption of the legend of St. George. But where do such expressions as "hoof and hellet" and "peg and wallet" come from?

At Peterboro' the dramatis personae consisted of three characters, but, unlike the play at Yaxley, unaccompanied by musicians. At least there was no instrumental music when Mr. Thompson played in it. The characters were King George, Beelzebub, and a Doctor. King George and the Doctor wore shirts adorned with a plentiful distribution of ribbons and coloured paper, while Beelzebub's proportions were considerably increased by a lavish stuffing of straw back and front.

The Mummers or Morris Dancers possessed good voices and musical knowledge, and the play was in all cases a prelude to the singing of songs and dancing. The songs sung were the current topical, comic, or pathetic songs of the day. The entertainment not uncommonly ended with the kitchen being cleared and the maid servants and others in the house joining the Morris Dancers in the old English country dances.

It is not difficult to understand that in days when there were no railways, no telegraphs, no cheap newspapers, "no nothings," as a famous humourist once expressed it, that the Morris Dancers were not unwelcome visitors in the sanded kitchens and parlours of country houses in the dark evenings of December, although the dialogue might not match that of "Ulysses".

Mr. Thompson says that before starting each evening certain houses were selected and enquiries made if Morris Dancing would be acceptable. On receiving an answer in the affirmative, the play commenced. At the close contributions were made, and the Mummers would receive between them about 20s. or 24s. each evening.

But let us reproduce the dialogue, quaint and crude as it is, as Mr. George Thompson remembers it

THE DOCTOR enters and says:

    In comes I who have never been before,
    Two more actors stand at the door.
    One can dance and one can sing,
    And by your leave one shall step in.

BEELZEBUB enters and says:

    In comes I old Beelzebub,

In my hand I carry my club,
Under my arm a dripping pan,
Don't you think I'm a jolly old man.
Beside I'm a little bold fellow,
What you please to call me, Punchinello.
I am huffed and puffed up like a fly,
From across the salt seas, above the lofty sky,
And the man who cannot fight,
Should neither live nor die.

KING GEORGE enters and says:

In comes I, King George the champion bold,
With my bright spear and bloody sword
I won three crowns of gold,
I fought a fiery dragon,
I brought him to the slaughter,
And by that means I won
The King of Egypt's daughter.
(Turning to the doctor.)
I am a King, I dare before you stand,
And I face you with my mighty hand.
I can hack you down and smack you
Small as flies,
And send you to Jamaica
To make mince pies.

THE DOCTOR:

You say you can hack me
And smack me
Small as flies,
And send me to Jamaica
To make mince pies
You roil my blood to say such thing
But I stand before you
Though you be a King.

THE KING:

King, King, or no King am I,
But you shall plainly see,
My sword's point shall answer thee.

THE DOCTOR:

My sword's point fears no art,
You and I will fight this out.

BEELZEBUB (parting them.)

Pooh, pooh, you foolish fellows,
What are you fighting for?

THE DOCTOR:

Honesty my good man.

BEELZEBUB:

Honesty be damned,
Never was their (*sic.*) honesty in my time.
You make your will before you die,
Lest you be as big a fool as I.
There's my sister Poll, and her hoof and hellet,
There's my broth er Dick, and his peg and wellet.
But I'm the eldest son amongst you all,
So draw your sword and let me fall.
(Falls to the ground as if dead.)

THE KING:

Oh see, oh see, what we have done,
We've slain our aged father
Before the rising sun.
See, how the blood streams on the floor,
I fear he never can rise more.
I'll give five pounds for a doctor.

THE DOCTOR:

I'd give ten pounds to keep away.

THE KING:

Fifteen pounds I'll give you.

THE DOCTOR:

I am a doctor – a doctor,
And have great skill
I can pluck that old chap's eye out
With a four-square ivory pill,
But the brain of a cart wheel
The skin of a live eel,
Two-pennyworth of tin tacks,
Two-pennyworth of round heads
Boil them all up together,
Put them on the old rogue's back
And he'll be ten times better
Than ever he was before.

THE KING:

Pray, sir, where did you receive your education?

THE DOCTOR:

In France and Spain and many a foreign nation.

THE KING:

Where did you travel from?

THE DOCTOR:

I travelled from the bed-side,
The fire-side, the cupboard-side,
That's where I've had many
A piece of cold potato pie,
And that's the truth, and no lie.
But pooh, pooh, you foolish fellow,
He is not dead, he's in a trance,
Rouse him up, and we will dance.
If we cannot dance,
We can sing,
So rouse him up,
And let's begin.

Then followed the singing and dancing.

Thomas Ratcliffe, 'Some Yule and New Year old customs'[7]

In comes I, Be-el-ze-bub,
Over my shoulder I carry my club;
In my hand a drippin' pan –
Don't you think I'm a jolly wo-man?

With such words, and as black as he is painted, "Devil Doubt" introduces himself at the close of the "guisers" play of "St. George," otherwise "The Pace Egg," the like of which will never be heard again as in the olden time of Christmas keeping. Why "Devil Doubt" should come in this at all at Christmastide, cannot readily be explained, except that the Devil is supposed to have a hand, or maybe only a finger, in the pie of mankind generally. The Devil cannot be kept out of things Christmassy, and in the mumming play he ends his share with the lines –

Money I want, money I'll have,
If you won't give me money,
I'll sweep you all to the grave.

In some cases this "Devil Doubt" carried a broom or a mop over his shoulder, and when thus armed the lines were more appropriate than when he carried a club. But in the mumming play there was much variety at the beginning, and also the ending, and of the

---

7   From the *Peterborough Advertiser,* 28 December 1908.

many times I have heard "St. George" I never heard two alike, and none which followed the play as published many years ago.

"Mummers," "Morris Dancers," or "Sword Dancers" are all but things of the past, and few perhaps now living have heard the music the "crowder" drew from his fiddle to which the morris or sword dancers timed their movements which were a real pleasure to look upon. The sword play could only be done in daylight, or in an ample-sized room well lighted, and this was perhaps the reason why, when night came, the performers turned themselves into waits or carol singers, for the old sort were masters of many parts in Christmas-keeping, not to forget their aptitude as trencher men when invited within, as they often were at the better houses in the Midlands and North-country parts.

Christmas-keeping at home has changed in many ways since the middle of last century, and there are now no cottage antics like there were in those days of home-made Christmas fare and home-brewed ale, wines, and that strange but taking mixture "posset," whose foundation was "nut-brown" or "elder-wine." The latter was the favourite drink every-where, no doubt because its fruit was from the tree so closely associated with the Saviour. I remember in some country places, where an elder tree was always a prominent feature in a cottage garden, hardly any would let a season pass without making elderberry wine, or elder syrup – the latter an unfailing remedy for coughs, colds, and throat ailments generally.

The cottager could not kill the fatted calf, but he did kill the fatted Christmas pig, out of which many sorts of Christmas cheer were made – "seam and chit'-lings" or "chitter-lings," as the more correct term. Then there were pies – pork and mince, sausage and black puddings, souce and savoury duck, all made in the best manner by the "mother of the house" and the daughters, if old enough, and vastly proud were they of their handiwork. But this is the middle of the fatted pig – the end came later in cutlets, or may-be a boiled or roast sucking pig's head.

Perhaps the most interesting item in the killing of the Christmas pig was the distribu-tion of the "pig's fry," which was cut up and sent on platters or plates covered with a white cloth to neighbours and friends. There was no robbing oneself in this fry distribution, for nearly everyone killed a pig just before Christmas, and all observed the custom that what went out came back in kind, and in return. The children were the carriers of the fry on behalf of their mothers, "Please, mother's sent this, and you mustn't wesh th'plate ner clout, or it will bring bad luck" – one way of disseminating folk-lore which hardly could be forgotten. I hope this happy custom still prevails in some country places.

The cottage Christmas parties were things once enjoyed, never forgotten. A blazing wood fire – a "Christmas Clog" in the middle, and lesser "logs" on each side, helped, with the long Christmas candles, the gift of the grocer, to well light the house-place, bedecked with red-berried holly and other evergreens, a gaily made kissing bush hanging from the house-beam – a thing made for use as well as ornament. The feast was continuous while the party lasted, the table loaded with good things standing as much out of the way as was possible to allow room for the games and rompings which took place, upon which the father and mother of the house looked with beaming faces.

The best of the New Year parties took place in the larger cottages, the tenant having a bit of land in his own cultivation, and being better able, though not more willing, than his less well-off neighbours. There was no question about the real enjoyment which was got out of these Christmas gatherings. There were always some who could tell a tale or give a doggerel song, or relate something about a ghost, the more hair-lifting the subject the better to like. Often there was the village fiddler asked in to help the singers along, to "crowder" a bit on his own account, or where there was room to play for a bit of dancing. Many and old fiddler could sing an old ballad, playing his own tune, by the way. Jokes were cracked, as well as nuts, and riddles propounded until the time came for parting. Before the parting came either the "good man" of the home or an appointed deputy would get on his legs and say the following, or something like it – for there were more than one rendering – known as

THE FOLKS

When me an' my folks
Come to see you an' your folks,
Let you an' your folks
Treat me an' my folks
As kind as me an' my folks
When you an' your folks
Came to see me an' my folks!
Sure there never were such folks
Since folks was folks!

It will be believed that such a "nominy" as "The Folks" could be gone through by few without a breakdown, and this caused much additional fun. Then "For he's a jolly good fellow" was gone through "at a ranting rate," and as the party broke up there were less "good nights."

Further details of the Peterborough mummers' play[8]

On this day [30 November] the Morris Dancers or Mummers began their visits. There were from four to eight people who took part in the Mummery. The King, Beelzebub, Doctor, Doctor's man and Jack, the fool. Sometimes one took the part of the Doctor's horse and the Doctor made his entry riding on the horse, who was on his hands and knees but he generally had a small stool in his hands to make him a little higher, when moving about.

---

8   From Dack (1911), p. 18.

Bibliography

Manuscript

Manuscript notes in the hand of Charles Dack in Cambridge University Library, Lib.5.89.520–1.

Printed sources

Adams, Theresa (2008) 'Representing rural leisure: John Clare and the politics of popular culture', *Studies in Romanticism,* 47, pp. 371–92.

Almond, Philip C. (2008) *The Witches of Warboys: An Extraordinary Story of Sorcery, Sadism and Satanic Possession.* London: I. B. Tauris.

Anlezark, Daniel (2013) 'The Anglo-Saxon world view', pp. 66–81 in M. Godden and M. Lapidge (eds), *The Cambridge Companion to Old English Literature,* 2nd edn. Cambridge: Cambridge University Press/

Aubrey, John (1696) *Miscellanies.* London.

Baker, A. E. (1854) *Glossary of Northamptonshire Words and Phrases,* 2 vols. London: J. R. Smith.

Barney, Shane M. (2005) 'The mythic matters of Edith Cavell: propaganda, legend, myth and memory', *Historical Reflections,* 31, pp. 217–33.

Barton, Anne (1999) 'Clare's animals: the wild and the tame', *John Clare Society Journal,* 18, pp. 5–22.

Belsey, Catherine (2010) 'Shakespeare's sad tale for winter: Hamlet and the tradition of fireside ghost stories', *Shakespeare Quarterly,* 61, pp. 1–27.

Borman, Tracy (2013) *Witches: A Tale of Sorcery, Scandal and Seduction.* London: Jonathan Cape.

Briggs, Katharine (2002) *The Fairies in Tradition and Literature.* London: Routledge (originally published 1967).

Bunch, Allan and Liquorice, Mary (1990) *Parish Churches in and around Peterborough.* Cambridge: Cambridgeshire Books.

CAMUS (2004) *Five Parishes, Their People and Places: A History of the Villages of Castor, Ailsworth, Marholm with Milton, Upton and Sutton.* Castor: CAMUS Project.

Cave, C. J. P. and Borenius, T. (1937) 'The painted ceiling in the nave of Peterborough Cathedral', *Archaeologia,* 88, pp. 297–309.

Chambers, E. K. (1933) *The English Folk-Play.* Oxford: Clarendon.

Chumbley, Andrew D. (2012) *The Leaper Between: An Historical Study of the Toad-bone Amulet.* Three Hands Press, https://threehandspress.com.

Clare, John (1996–2003) *Poems of the Middle Period: 1822–1837,* ed. E. Robinson, D. Powell and P. M. S. Dawson, 5 vols. Oxford: Clarendon.

Clare, John (2002) *John Clare by Himself,* ed. E. Robinson and D. Powell, 2nd edn. New York: Routledge.

Clark, C. (ed.) (1958) *The Peterborough Chronicle, 1070–1154.* Oxford: Oxford University Press.

Clarke, Basil (1975) *Mental Disorder in Earlier Britain: Exploratory Studies.* Cardiff: University of Wales Press.

Clive-Rouse, Edward and Baker, Audrey (1955) 'The wall-paintings at Longthorpe Tower, near Peterborough', *Archaeologia,* 116, pp. 1–57.

Codd, Daniel (2009) *Mysterious Northamptonshire.* Derby: Breedon Books.

Craddock, Thomas (1864) *Peterborough Cathedral: A General, Architectural, and Monastic History*. Peterborough: J. S. Clarke.

Dack, Charles (1899) 'Old Peterborough customs and their survival', *Journal of the British Archaeological Association*, New Series 5, pp. 323–42.

Dack, Charles (1903) 'A forgotten festival', *The Golden Penny*, 28 November, p. 431.

Dack, Charles (1911) *Weather and Folk Lore of Peterborough and District*. Peterborough: Peterborough Natural History, Scientific, and Archaeological Society.

Darby, H. C. (1936) *An Historical Geography of England before A.D. 1800*. Cambridge: Cambridge University Library.

Davidson, Thomas (1956–7) 'The horseman's word: a rural initiation ceremony', *Gwerin: A Half-Yearly Journal of Folklore*, 1, pp. 67–74.

Davies, A. (1989) 'Witches in Anglo-Saxon England: five case histories', pp. 41–56 in D. G. Scragg (ed.), *Superstition and Popular Medicine in Anglo-Saxon England*. Manchester: Manchester University Press.

Davies, Owen (2003) *Popular Magic: Cunning-folk in English History*. London: Continuum.

Davies, Reginald Trevor *(1947) Four Centuries of Witch Beliefs, with special reference to the Great Rebellion*. London: Methuen.

Deacon, George (1983) *John Clare and the Folk Tradition*. London: Sinclair Browne.

Defoe, Daniel (1748) *A Tour thro' the whole Island of Great Britain* , 4 vols. London.

Dillinger, Johannes (2012) *Magical Treasure Hunting in Europe and North America: A History*. London: Palgrave Macmillan.

Dixon, George (1980) *Old Scarlett*. Peterborough: Annakin.

Dugdale, William (1655) *Monasticon Anglicanum*, 3 vols. London.

Dunn, Marilyn (2009) *The Christianization of the Anglo-Saxons c. 597–c. 700: Discourses of Life, Death and Afterlife*. London: Continuum.

Eastern Angles (2016)*Eastern Angles in Peterborough: 2008–2016 and beyond*. Peterborough.

Elmer, Peter (2016) *Witchcraft, Witch-hunting and Politics in Early Modern England*. Oxford: Oxford University Press.

Fairweather, Janet (ed.) (2005) *Liber Eliensis: A History of the Isle of Ely from the Seventh Century to the Twelfth*. Woodbridge: Boydell.

Ferreiro, Alberto (2005) *Simon Magus in Patristic, Medieval and Early Modern Traditions*. Leiden, Netherlands: Brill.

Fincham, Kenneth (2004) 'Dove, Thomas (1555–1630), bishop of Peterborough, pp. 757–8 in *The Oxford Dictionary of National Biography*, vol. 16. Oxford: Oxford University Press.

Foot, Sarah (2006) *Monastic Life in Anglo-Saxon England, c. 600–900*. Cambridge: Cambridge University Press.

Foreman, Paul (2015) *The Cambridge Book of Magic: A Tudor Necromancer's Manual*, ed. F. Young. Cambridge: Texts in Early Modern Magic.

Friis-Jensen, K. and Willoughby, J. M. W. (eds) (2001), *Peterborough Abbey*, Corpus of British Medieval Library Catalogues 8. London: British Academy.

L. G. (1901) 'The Liberty of Peterborough', *Fenland Notes and Queries*, 5, pp. 355–60.

Gerald of Wales (1978) *The Journey through Wales and the Description of Wales*, trans. L. Thorpe. Harmondsworth: Penguin.

Gerould, Gordon Hall (1917) 'The legend of St. Wulfhad and St. Ruffin at Stone Priory', *Proceedings of the Modern Language Association*, 32, pp. 323–37.

Ginzberg, Carlo (1983) *The Night Battles: Witchcraft and Agrarian Cults in the Sixteenth and Seventeenth Centuries*. London: Routledge & Kegan Paul.

Gollin, Alfred (1989) *The Impact of Air Power on the British People and Their Government, 1909–1914./* Stanford, Calif.: Stanford University Press.

Gransden, Antonia (2007) *A History of the Abbey of Bury St Edmunds 1182–1256.* Woodbridge: Boydell.

Grummett, David (2016) *Material Eucharist.* Oxford: Oxford University Press.

Gunton, Symon (1686) *The History of the Church of Peterburgh,* ed. Simon Patrick.

Hall, Alaric (2007) 'Glosses, gaps and gender: the rise of female elves in Anglo-Saxon Culture', pp. 139–70 in M. Risannen, M. Hintikka, L. Kahlas-Tarkka and R. McConchie (eds), *Change in Meaning and the Meaning of Change: Studies in Semantics and Grammar from Old to Present-day English.* Helsinki: Société Néophilologique.

Hall, David (1987) *The Fenland Project, Number 2: Fenland Landscapes and Settlement between Peterborough and March.* Cambridge: Cambridgeshire Archaeological Committee.

Hall, Jackie and Wright, Susan M. (eds) (2015) *Conservation and Discovery: Peterborough Cathedral Nave Ceiling and Related Structures.* London: Museum of London Archaeology.

Halliday, Robert (2010) 'The roadside burial of suicides: an East Anglian Study', *Folklore,* 121, pp. 81–93.

Halpin, Patricia A. (1997) 'Anglo-Saxon women and pilgrimage', pp. 97–122 in Christopher Harper-Bill (ed.), *Anglo-Norman Studies, 19: Proceedings of the Battle Conference 1996.* Woodbridge: Boydell Press.

Hardy, T. D. and Martin, C. T. (eds) (1888) *Gesta Herwardi incliti exulis et militis,* in Geoffroy Gaimar, *Lestorie des Engles,* vol. 1. London: Her Majesty's Stationery Office.

Harms, D., Clark, J. R. and Peterson, J. H. (eds) (2015) *The Book of Oberon: A Sourcebook of Elizabethan Magic.* Woodbury, Minn.: Llewellyn.

Harpsfield, Nicholas (1622) *Historia Anglicana ecclesiastica.* Douai, France.

Henderson, George (1981) 'The damnation of Nero and related themes', pp. 39–51 in A. Borg and A. Martindale (eds), *The Vanishing Past: Studies in Medieval Art, Liturgy and Metrology presented to Christopher Hohler.* Oxford: Oxford University Press.

Herbert, Kathleen (1994) *Looking for the Lost Gods of England.* Swaffham: Anglo-Saxon Books.

Heylyn, Peter (1652) *Cosmographie.* London.

Higham, Jack (1988) 'The cult of St. Oswald at Peterborough', *Peterborough's Past,* 3, pp. 15–22.

Hill, Peter (2005) *Folklore of Northamptonshire.* Stroud: History Press.

Hough, Carole (2014) *'An Ald Reht': Essays on Anglo-Saxon Law.* Newcastle-upon-Tyne: Cambridge Scholars Publishing.

Houghton[-Walker], Sarah (2006) 'The "community" of John Clare's Helpston', *Studies in English Literature, 1500–1900,* 46, pp. 781–802.

Houghton-Walker, Sarah (2009) *John Clare's Religion.* Farnham: Ashgate.

Huntington, Joanna (2013) '"The quality of his virtus proved him a perfect man": Hereward "the Wake" and the representation of lay masculinity', pp. 77–93 in P. H. Cullum and K. J. Lewis (eds), *Religious Men and Masculine Identity in the Middle Ages.* Woodbridge: Boydell Press.

Hutton, Ronald (1991) *The Pagan Religions of the Ancient British Isles: Their Nature and Legacy.* Oxford: Blackwell.

Hutton, Ronald (1996) *The Stations of the Sun: A History of the Ritual Year in Britain .* Oxford: Oxford University Press.

James, Maureen (2012) 'The Peterborough Folk Club Mummers Play – an interesting history', paper given at Mummers Unconvention, Bath, 16 November.

James, Maureen (2014) *Cambridgeshire Folk Tales.* Stroud: History Press.

James, M. R. (1894–98) 'On the paintings formerly in the Choir at Peterborough', *Proceedings of the Cambridge Antiquarian Society,* 9, pp. 178–94.

Jansen, Annemiek (1995) 'The fevelopment of the St Oswald legends on the continent' , pp. 230–40 in Claire Stancliffe and Eric Cambridge (eds), *Oswald: Northumbrian King to European Saint.* Stamford: Paul Watkins.

Janson, H. W. (1952) *Apes and Ape Lore in the Middle Ages and the Renaissance.* London: Warburg Institute.

Jones, Brian (2014) *The Peterborough Book of Days.* Stroud: History Press.

Journal of the Northamptonshire Natural History Society and Field Club (1925) 'A witch at Peterborough', 22, p. 224.

Kama, Shama and Whomsley, Stuart (2011) *Working with Pakistani Service Users and Their Families: A Practitioner's Guide.* Cambridgeshire and Peterborough NHS Foundation Trust.

Kay, Emma (2015) *Dining with the Victorians: A Delicious History.* Stroud: Amberley.

Kingsley, Charles (1866) *Hereward: The Last of the English.* Boston, Mass.: Ticknor & Fields.

Kittredge, George Lyman (1928) *Witchcraft in Old and New England.* Cambridge, Mass.: Harvard University Press.

Klaniczay, Gábor (2002) *Holy Rulers and Blessed Princesses: Dynastic Cults in Medieval Central Europe.* Cambridge: Cambridge University Press.

Knights, Mark (2011) *The Devil in Disguise: Deception, Delusion and Fanaticism in the Early English Enlightenment.* Oxford: Oxford University Press.

Knowles, David (1963) *The Monastic Order in England,* 2nd edn. Cambridge: Cambridge University Press.

Lapidge, M., Blair, J., Keynes, S. and Scragg, D. (eds), (2000) *The Blackwell Encyclopedia of Anglo-Saxon England.* Oxford: Blackwell.

Lewis, Robert E. (ed.) (1952–2001) *Middle English Dictionary,* 118 vols. Ann Arbor, Mich.: University of Michigan Press.

Lines, Rodney (1986) 'John Clare and herbal medicine', *John Clare Society Journal,* 5, pp. 16–21.

Luxford, Julian (2015) 'Intelligent by design: the manuscripts of Walter of Whittlesey, monk of Peterborough', *Electronic British Library Journal,* pp. 1–33.

Meaney, A. L. (1966) 'Woden in England: a reconsideration of the evidence', *Folklore,* 77, pp. 105–15.

Mellows, W. T. (ed.) (1937) *Peterborough Local Administration: Minutes and Accounts of the Feoffees and Governors of the City Lands,* Northamptonshire Records Society 10. Kettering: Northamptonshire Record Society.

Milis, Ludo (2012) 'The spooky heritage of ancient paganisms', pp. 1–18 in C. Steel, J. Marenbon and W. Verbeke (eds), *Paganism in the Middle Ages: Threat and Fascination.* Leuven, Neths: Leuven University Press.

Morton, John (1712) *The Natural History of Northampton-shire; with some account of the antiquities.* London.

Nordström, Folke (1955) 'Peterborough, Lincoln and the science of Robert Grosseteste: a study in thirteenth century architecture and iconography', *Art Bulletin,* 37, pp. 241–72.

North, Richard (1997) *Heathen Gods in Old English Literature.* Cambridge: Cambridge University Press.

Oldridge, Darren (2010) *The Devil in Tudor and Stuart England,* 2nd edn. Stroud: History Press.

Orme, Stuart (2012) *Haunted Peterborough.* Stroud: History Press.

Palmer, Martin and Palmer, Nigel (2000) *The Spiritual Traveller: England, Scotland, Wales: The Guide to Sacred Sites and Pilgrim Routes in Britain*. Mahwah, N.J.: HiddenSpring.

Parish, R. B. (2002) 'The Holy Well, or St Cloud's Well, at Longthorpe Park near Peterborough', *Living Spring Journal*, 2 (November), people.bath.ac.uk/liskmj/living-spring/journal/issue2/dipping/rparlon1.htm

Pattison, G. W. (1953) 'Adult education and folklore', *Folklore*, 64, pp. 424–6.

Perry, Stephen (1992) *A Nostalgic Journey through Garton End*. Peterborough.

Pinner, Rebecca (2015) *The Cult of St Edmund in Medieval East Anglia*. Woodbridge: Boydell & Brewer.

Pluskowski, Aleksander (2006) *Wolves and Wilderness in the Middle Ages*. Woodbridge: Boydell Press.

Porter, Enid (1961) 'Folk life and traditions of the Fens', *Folklore*, 72, pp. 584–98.

Porter, Enid (1969) *Cambridgeshire Customs and Folklore*. London: Routledge & Kegan Paul.

Pownall, Thomas (1788–89a) 'Observations on the origin and progress of Gothic architecture, and on the Corporation of Free Masons supposed to be the establishers of it as a regular order', *Archaeologia* 9, pp. 110–26.

Pownall, Thomas(1788–89b) 'Observations on ancient painting in England. In a letter from Gov. Pownall, to the Rev. Michael Lort, D. D. V. P. A. S.', *Archaeologia*, 9 pp. 141–56.

Prior, Avril Lumley (2008) 'Fact and/or folklore? The case for St Pega of Peakirk', *Northamptonshire Past and Present*, 61, pp. 7–16.

Reliquary (1885) 'Parish Registers of St. John the Baptist, Peterborough and Holy Cross Westgate, Canterbury', *The Reliquary*, 26 (October), pp. 83–5.

Robinson, Eric (2013) 'John Clare: games, pastimes, sports and customs', *Wordsworth Circle*, 44, pp. 56–60.

Rollason, David (1995) 'St Oswald in post-Conquest England', pp. 164–77 in Claire Stancliffe and Eric Cambridge (eds), *Oswald: Northumbrian King to European Saint*. Stamford: Paul Watkins.

Rooney, Anne (1993) *The Hunt in Middle English Literature* . Cambridge: D. S. Brewer.

Rosen, Barbara (ed.) (1991) *Witchcraft in England, 1558–1618*. Amherst, Mass.: University of Massachusetts Press.

Rositzke, H. A. (ed. and trans.) (1951) *The Peterborough Chronicle*. New York: Columbia University Press.

Roud, Steve (2006) *The English Year: A month-by-month guide to the nation's customs and festivals, from May Day to Mischief Night*. London: Penguin.

Ryan, J. S. (1963) 'Othin in England: evidence from the poetry for a cult of Woden in Anglo-Saxon England', *Folklore*, 74, pp. 460–80.

Saunders, W. H. Bernard (1888) *Legends and Traditions of Huntingdonshire*. Peterborough: George Caster.

Serjeantson, R. M. and Adkins, William Ryland D. (eds) (1906) *The Victoria History of the County of Northampton*, vol. 2. London: Archibald Constable.

Smith, J. B. (1990) 'John Clare's constellations', *John Clare Society Journal*, 9, pp. 5–13.

Sollerio, J. B., Pinio, J., Cupero, G. and Boschio, P. (eds) (1727) *Acta Sanctorum Iulii* , vol. 5. Antwerp, Belgium.

Srivastava, Vinay K. (1988) 'Ethnographic notebook: modern witchcraft and occultism in Cambridge', *Cambridge Journal of Anthropology*, 13, pp. 50–71.

Stenton, F. M. (1943) 'The historical bearing of place-name studies: the place of women in Anglo-Saxon society', *Transactions of the Royal Historical Society*, 25, pp. 1–13.

Sternberg, Thomas (1851) *The Dialect and Folk-lore of Northamptonshire*. London: J. R. Smith.

Story, Alfred T. (1883) *Historical Legends of Northhamptonshire*. Northampton: John Taylor.

Swain, E. G. (2009) *The Stoneground Ghost Tales*. Cambridge: Oleander Press.

Tebbutt, C. F. (1952) *Huntingdonshire Folklore*. St Ives: privately published.

Thomas, Keith (1991) *Religion and the Decline of Magic*, 2nd edn. Harmondsworth: Penguin.

Thompson, Beeby (1913), 'Peculiarities of waters and wells', *Journal of the Northamptonshire Natural History Society and Field Club*, 17, pp. 101–15.

Trehane, Emma (2005) '"Emma and Johnny": the friendship between Eliza Emmerson and John Clare', *John Clare Society Journal*, 24, pp. 69–77.

Turner, William (1697) *A compleat history of the most remarkable providences both of judgment and mercy, which have hapned in this present age*. London.

Vince, A. G. (1990) *Saxon London: An Archaeological Investigation*. London: Seaby.

Watson, Nigel (2015) *UFOs of the First World War: Phantom Airships, Balloons, Aircraft and Other Mysterious Aerial Phenomena*. Stroud: History Press.

Wertheimer, Laura (2006) 'Clerical dissent, popular piety, and sanctity in fourteenth-century Peterborough: the cult of Laurence of Oxford', *Journal of British Studies*, 45, pp. 3–25.

Westwood, Jennifer and Simpson, Jacqueline (2005) *The Lore of the Land: A Guide to England's Legends, from Spring-Heeled Jack to the Witches of Warboys*. London: Penguin.

Whitelock, Dorothy (ed.) (1953) *English Historical Documents, c. 500–1042*. London: Eyre & Spottiswoode.

Wise, Charles (1905) *Northamptonshire Legends put into Rhyme*. Kettering/

Young, Francis (ed.) (2016a) *A Medieval Book of Magical Stones: The Peterborough Lapidary*. Cambridge: Texts in Early Modern Magic.

Young, Francis (2016b) *The Abbey of Bury St Edmunds: History, Legacy and Discovery*. Norwich: Lasse Press.

Yun, Bee (2007) 'A visual mirror of princes: the wheel on the mural of Longthorpe Tower', *Journal of the Warburg and Courtauld Institutes*, 70, pp. 1–32.

Yun, Bee (2015) 'The representation of an Indian prince in the Great Chamber of Longthorpe Tower and the intercultural transfer of political ideas in the Middle Ages', *Notes in the History of Art*, 34, pp. 1–6.

Newspapers[1]

Cambridge Independent Press
11 May 1844

Lincolnshire Chronicle
11 May 1849

Liverpool Daily Post
19 November 1867

Peterborough Advertiser
12 March 1902

---

1   Many of the newspaper cuttings in Charles Dack's collection are either undated or the newspaper is unidentified. Only when the title and date of an article is known is it given here, otherwise it is cited in the text with the MS page number it is assigned in Dack's volume.

23 April 1902
5 March 1904
28 December 1908
6 May 1911
17 May 1911
9 November 1911

Peterborough Standard
10 February 1912

Saturday Citizen
2 December 1905
14 January 1911

Web resources

British Museum collections online, britishmuseum.org/research/collection_online
Electronic British Library Journal, bl.uk/eblj
Folklore Society, folklore-society.com
Langdyke Countryside Trust, langdyke.org.uk
Living Spring Journal, people.bath.ac.uk/liskmj/living-spring/journal
Metropolitan Museum of Art, metmuseum.org
Office for National Statistics, visual.ons.gov.uk
Peterborough City Council, peterborough.gov.uk
Peterborough Telegraph, online edition, peterboroughtoday.co.uk
Umilta website, umilta.net

Index

For ease of identification, names of places now located within Peterborough Unitary Authority are given with the ancient county in which they were once located, i.e. Northants, Hunts or Cambs. Note that some sources will now locate all of these places in the modern, much enlarged ceremonial county of Cambridgeshire.

Notes are indicated by 'n.', and references to illustrations are in **bold**.

Francis Young was born and educated in Bury St Edmunds and obtained his PhD in History from Cambridge University. He is the author of numerous books on East Anglian history including *Where is St Edmund?* (2014), *The Gages of Hengrave and Suffolk Catholicism* (2015), *Rookwood Family Papers* (2016) and the official history of the Roman Catholic Diocese of East Anglia, *Catholic East Anglia* (2016). He has written two books for the Lasse Press. He lives in Peterborough with his wife and daughter.

By the same author

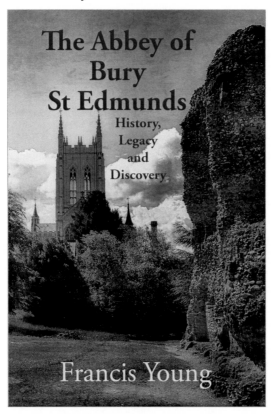

The Abbey of St Edmund was founded around the relics of St Edmund, king and martyr, patron saint of England in the Middle Ages, and grew to be one of the great religious establishments of medieval England. Among the many influential monks was the poet John Lydgate. Relations with the town the Abbey dominated and controlled were often far from easy, and at times exploded into violence. A disastrous fire, and the collapse of the great tower, were among the catastrophes the monks had to endure, yet the Abbey became a European centre of art, culture and learning. This is the first complete history of the Abbey from foundation to dissolution.

Contents:
A timeline of St Edmunds Abbey; Introduction; Origins, 869–1065; The Golden Age: from Baldwin to Anselm, 1065–1148; The age of Samson and the age of Magna Carta, 1148–1229; A century of troubles, 1229–1329; Plague, revolt and fire, 1329–1469; The final years, 1469–1539; Legacy; Discovery; Appendices: Abbots, Priors and Sacrists; A guided tour of the Abbey Church in 1465; Bibliography; Index.

Also from the Lasse Press

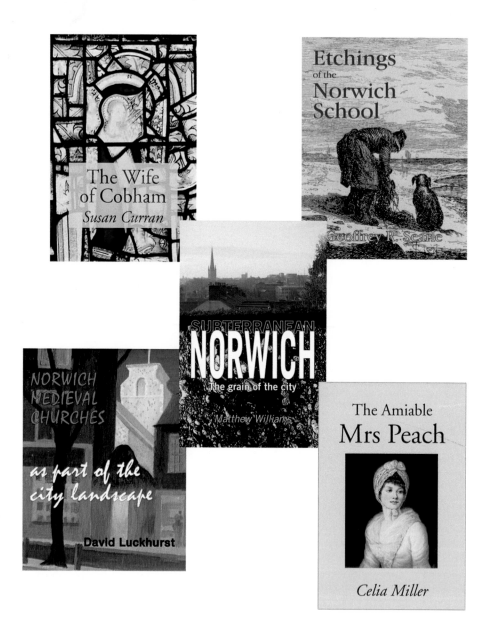

Details of all our titles are available on

www.lassepress.com